Military Ethics

Attention Authors

'We Convert Fighters into Writers'. That's the motto of Manas Publications since more than four decades. Our message to the world is that India can win the battle not only by the bullet but also by the pen. There is no dearth of intellectuals in our country, but their knowledge is confined to them only. No sincere effort has been made by any other publisher to channelise their knowledge in national interest. That is why the talent of a large number of intellectuals remains latent. An author transforms his knowledge into a manuscript, and it is our job to spread his/her knowledge by converting it into a beautiful book. For over four decades, Manas has been motivating the intellectuals by publishing their manuscripts and would like to publish your manuscript too. If you or your colleagues have any manuscript ready for publication or are working on it, kindly contact us with detailed synopsis and list of contents. We will transform your work into a valuable publication. If you wish, we can also suggest you the suitable subjects for writing the books related to your area of expertise. Manas is known for its publishing quality and commitments. We take utmost care in production and give wide publicity to the book as well as its author through our national and international distribution network.

Military Ethics

Lt Gen SRR Aiyengar
PVSM, AVSM, VSM (Retd)

Manas Publications
(We Convert Fighters into Writers)
New Delhi-110002 (INDIA)

MANAS PUBLICATIONS
(We Convert Fighters into Writers)
(Publishers, Library Suppliers, Importers & Exporters)
4402/5-A, Ansari Road (Opp. HDFC Bank)
Darya Ganj, New Delhi - 110 002 (India)
Phones: Off.: 011-23260783, 23265523, Res.: 011-23842660
E-mail : manaspublications@gmail.com
manaspub6@gmail.com
Website : www.manaspublications.in

ISBN 978-81-7049-504-8

595/-

Designed at
Veronica Grafic Arts

Printed in India at
R.K. Printers, Delhi
Published by Mrs Suman Lata for
Manas Publications
4402/5-A, Ansari Road (Opp HDFC Bank)
Darya Ganj, New Delhi - 110 002 (INDIA)

Contents

Part 3: Miscellaneous Issues impacting Ethics

Expert Opinions

1. *"I have gone through your book on Military Ethics and found it be interesting and reminiscent of our great ancient culture.*

2. *Our Founding Fathers mainly based the great Constitution on our lasting culture, which has indeed sustained the Nation. The preamble itself lays down the Goal-to constitute India into a Sovereign, Socialist, Secular, Democratic Republic. Article 51 A sets down the fundamental duties of a citizen, which among other things focuses on abidance by the Constitution, protection of the Sovereignty, Unity and Integrity of India, defence of the country, and promotion of harmony. The manner expected of functioning of the ieople, and naturally of the disciplined Armed Forces, is therefore absolutely clear.*

3. *Duty, Righteousness (Dharma), and Ethics are really part and parcel of our great Constitution. While professionalism and character are essential in everyone, for the Armed Forces these are vital. In your book, you have obviously taken a lot of trouble in analyzing the importance of Ethics, what all it constitutes, applicability to everyone and particularly the military, positive and negative aspects of its implementation, guidelines provided, and many other useful recommendations.*

4. *I trust that people, particularly the military, will make a careful study of your book, comprehend the important aspects and implement to the maximum extent in their normal life, for the good of the Nation. I hope, it inspires many to rethink what holds the Nation together, and what holds the personnel of the Armed Forces together."*

General KVKrishna Rao, PVSM (Retd)

Former Chief of Army Staff & Chairman Chiefs of Staff, Governor of Nagaland, Manipur, Tripura & Mizoram, Jammu & Kashmir.

"In a bleak environment of moral decline, as we watch India's, once respected, institutions tumble in succession, Lt. Gen. SRR Aiyengar has rendered yeoman service by, sharing with us, his reflections on Military Ethics. While holding up a mirror before all of us, the author points out the challenges and pitfalls that face military leaders in particular; signposting the ethical options available and gently urging us to seek solutions from within our profound but neglected cultural heritage. A valuable compendium of essays, speeches and ruminations, by a soldier-scholar, which provides food for thought in our troubled times."

Admiral Arun Prakash (Retd)

PVSM, AVSM. VrC, VSM

Former Chief of the Naval Staff.

Foreword

Our Armed Forces 'exist to fight and win', so as to enforce peace, whenever and wherever called upon to do so. For this they must be 'ever prepared and powerful'- 'sarvada shaktishali'. Such 'Shakti' comes not just from the 'physical, mental and technological strengths' but from the 'Spirit' that manifests as 'Espirit de Corps/ Regimental Spirit'. The bonding of the 'Brothers in Arms' is not by 'gold or gongs' but by higher values of 'Truth, Trust and Dharma (Righteous Duty).' The 'essence' of Military Leadership is 'spiritual'- take that away and you will be left with a 'shav'.

Ethical values are, therefore, imperatives of 'our existence'– not a cosmetic optional extra! It is in this context that Lt Gen Aiyengar, who enjoys an enviable reputation as a 'Scholar-Soldier', has come up with this work of great merit and meaning. He is essentially urging the readers to contemplate on the 'ethical obligations' of their professional calling. He has presented a 'way of thinking' about leadership rather than any 'prescriptive solutions'. By reflecting over his thoughts, leaders can test their sense of moral seriousness and public purpose. This book explores ideas that anchor 'professional military service' to fundamental beliefs of 'human value and dignity'. In the process, the author is hoping to engage all military professionals in serious 'professional introspection'.

I am happy that his book also highlights aspects of traditional Indian wisdom such as the role of TRIGUNAS- the three basic 'qualitative' constituents of Creation- also referred to as PRAKRITI/NATURE- viz, SATTVA (Goodness), RAJAS (Passion) and TAMAS (Ignorance). It is a mix of these that determines the personality- orientation and character of an individual, and hence, his behavior as a leader. These are not attributes or qualities but one's essential (spiritual) nature. It is my belief that these aspects have not been fully explored or exploited as a matrix for leadership selection and development, perhaps, because these are Indian and ancient. Ranga Aiyengar has taken a bold step on this promising path of re-discovery of our ancient wisdom by suggesting the scope of correlations between 'gunas- leadership ethics/imperatives- related HR systems'. Hopefully someone will follow up.

The issues addressed in the book are complex and thinking people may disagree about many aspects. If it stimulates thoughtful discussion amongst military professionals it will have served its purpose.

It has been a privilege to contribute this Foreword. For this I am grateful to the Author and wish him the very best.

Lt Gen YN Sharma, PVSM, AVSM, VSM (Retired)

Former General Officer Commanding in Chief

Ex Colonel THE GRENADIERS

Acknowledgement

Writing a book is often described as a lonely effort, but in reality my journey would not have been possible without a host of my supporters behind the scene.

I would like to thank my friend, philosopher and guide, Professor Kittu Reddy of Sri Aurobindo Ashram for sharing his thoughts on Ethics, Morality, Character and Leadership. Right from his childhood days spent in the Divine care of Mother at the Ashram, he has been closely associated with the three Services in conducting workshops at various training establishments and formations. A constant message that comes out from his talks is that, *"Only recourse is to strengthen and internalize the values one would like to develop. In simple words this can only be done by 'knowing oneself'. It is not enough to follow the education system as it is practiced now, but to add to it the element of self-knowledge in the system. This has to be done not only in the schools, but in the family and all other fields and areas."*

I am also indebted to my mentor, Lt Gen Y.N. Sharma, PVSM, AVSM, VSM (Retd) - former General Officer Commanding in Chief and ex- Colonel THE GRENADIERS, for his constant encouragement and sharing his views on various issues addressed in the book. He is a true 'Karma yogi', and his intense and abiding faith in '*Sanatana Dharma*'

(Eternal Religion) is, indeed, very admirable. True ethics, in his opinion, is Dharma-the right fulfillment and working of the higher nature. It is this inspiration which prompted me to include in my book an article on *'Ancient Indian Ethos and its Discourse on Ethics'*. A true believer in Vedanta's mental temperament of human beings (*GUNAS*), and its practical application in evaluating the character of an individual to forewarn possible ethical failings.

On a personal level, I would like to place on record the unflagging support and love of my wife Subhashini, for her insistence on my writing this book. I also realized, as I set upon this task, that her constant companionship over all these years has been the inspiration to lead a happy and contended life ethically. She made it worth it, each and every moment. I would be failing in my duty if I did not acknowledge the help of my loving and affectionate daughter Sonia and grandson Viraj, who with their infinite patience and sharp and watchful eyes, scanned the text and removed a host of anomalies that had existed before it went for publication.

The author wishes to thank the Chief/Managing editors of *The War College Journal*, *Journal of Defence Studies*, and *TRISHUL*-The Tri-Service Professional Journal, for permission accorded to reproduce my articles/essays earlier published in their Journals.

I would like to place on record my very sincere appreciation for the painstaking and prompt secretarial assistance extended by Shri Gopal Malo and Shri Kiran Kumar in compiling this book. He was indeed a great help.

Finally, I would like to thank the staff of *MANAS* Publications, for all the help and co-operation in bringing out this book.

Introduction

The ethical obligations of the officer are objective and are not contingent on any desire held by any individual. The professional military ethic is not a relative ethic. The obligation to uphold it or any of its tenets does not arise because those in the profession said so, but rather, because it is necessary if the profession is to be effective in its purpose of war fighting. In a relativist ethic what is good or bad is justified based on the desires of the individual or group; what is good is what makes one (or the group) feel good, while what is bad is what does not. For a professional ethic, good and bad are determined, in part functionally, by how the profession contributes to society. The military performs a socially useful, indeed, vital function - the protection of Society, its territory and way of life. This creates a moral obligation for the soldier, particularly for the commissioned officer, to respond effectively when called on to defend a defenseless society, even to the point of death.[1]

It is true that we have been under sustained battering in the media about a series of incidents and allegations regarding senior and middle level officers involved in various acts of alleged impropriety. The general reaction to

1. Samuel Huntington, The Soldier and the State, New Haven: Harvard University Press, 1957, Chapter 3.

the whole mess is anger, dismay, and exasperation at the activities of a handful of individuals who have smeared the otherwise highly positive public image of the armed forces painfully built and maintained by the achievements and sacrifices of successive generations of our men and commanders.

Public images and organizational reputations are fragile and perishable entities and their upkeep requires a colossal and never-ending effort. This is especially so in the case of the Indian Army, whose reputation is built on the irreplaceable foundations of soldiers lost in battles. The traditional argument sometimes advanced is that the Services are a microcosm of contemporary society, and thus, reflect its failings and shortcomings. This argument must not be stretched too far. It is true, that our Services springs from within the Indian society and is a people's armed force in every sense of the term; but its way of life, developed and nurtured across a span of over two centuries, makes it distinctive and quite different from the civil society in the country. It is based on conscious adherence to values, ethics, and a code of conduct which have long been diluted elsewhere. Such a dilution cannot be allowed in the Services too.

It is, meanwhile, imperative for us to put our house in order, for which it has or must have already taken appropriate action. A dispassionate self-appraisal is necessary to determine what further steps are required to apply the brakes on this apparently runaway train of criminal irresponsibility. However, the understandable urge for damage control on a crash action basis must not be allowed to short circuit the due process of military procedure and law. Even under these challenging circumstances, commanders must stand their ground against political and bureaucratic heckling and avoid precipitate actions of 'kangaroo' court justice.

Defense Services, for historical and socio-political reasons, have an exalted position in the Indian society. Their leadership will always be held to a higher, exacting standard of values because the society and the nation sees the civil society as more dishonest, self-indulgent, more corrupt, more disloyal, less disciplined, and more materialistic than military culture. The burden of these expectations as well as the cost of being different from (and superior) to a civilian, cannot be dissociated from the honor, respect, and privileges which come with donning the military uniform.

Chips and flakes of plaster may sometimes have been knocked off the structure, but the underlying masonry has always remained solid, reliable, and enduring. The armed forces largely continue to be regarded by the country as its favorite son, and it is precisely for this very reason, the organization's conduct in war and peace should remain impeccably correct at all times. Though adverse publicity has put the Services on few occasions on the defensive at present, it must still be careful to think through its proposed remedial actions. Those who transgress the accepted norms must be taken to task by due process of military law. Retribution must visit the wrongdoers, but again, only after diligence. The stakes are just too high for anything else.

The very fact that we are paying greater attention to the ethical dimensions of leadership has helped to improve the internal health of the Army, as a former Chief of the Army Staff (COAS) remarked. It has allowed for introspection and set the debate amongst the rank and file. A large number of tangible and intangible things have happened. We ensured that greater probity and transparency was stressed and greater awareness to imbibe service ethos was brought in. What became clear to all was that we would not desist from taking appropriate action against anyone. At the same time we must understand that in one go, one cannot bring about total change, but the process has started and I am confident that things will look up.

PART-I

Ethical Dimensions of Military Leadership

1

Ethics and Military Leadership*

"Yat-Yat acarati sresthas – tat-tad eve'taro janah
Sa yat pranam kurute---lokas tad anuvartate"

(Whichever may be the way of life that a superior adopts – that very one is by other people (followed). What he makes his guiding principle, the world too behaves even according to the same."

The Bhagavad Gita, Chapter Three, Verse 21

(*Essay published in 'Journal of Defence Studies , Volume 7, Number 2, April-June 2013,pp 121-142.A quarterly, research periodical published by the Institute for Defence Studies and Analysis, New Delhi.)

Introduction

The question of ethics is faced in all walks of life. Everywhere it raises hard, often insoluble, questions about the choice of the right path. This is probably one of the most difficult areas to define in any profession. Such normative judgments can never have universal applications; additionally, they may be time specific. What may have been the right thing to do in one age or at a certain point of time may be totally wrong in another. Parties with perfectly clear consciences may often choose radically different paths. However, core values of any organization do not change with times or people. Core values are those that govern personal relationships, clarify who we are, articulate what we stand for, guide us how to teach, show us how to reward, and guide us in making decisions. In other words, the essential tenets of an organization and are the practices we use (or should be using) everyday, in everything we do.

The bigger hurdle even to a sincere wish to conform to ethical principles is the persistent cropping up of situations where ethical principles themselves may be contradictory and one has to make a difficult choice, guided by one's conscience. Conscience is probably best described as a fallible moral judgment which, if acknowledged, produces actions and which if ignored, merely produces guilt. An informed ethical conscience consistent with value systems strengthens a leader to make right choices when faced with tough issues. Ethics is ultimately about individual character as manifested in the decisions and actions of all who are considered leaders within the profession. Leadership is best understood as a matter of character that demands individual moral decisions. Its exercise can never be a mindless application of popular and simplistic formulae.

In the relentless quest for success, recognition and even fame in an increasingly consumerist competitive world, we all seem to have become obsessed with 'doing the thing right' rather than 'doing the right thing'. Intense competition to climb the 'pyramid', numerous environmental compulsions and the desire for quick results in the face of complex pressures have possibly resulted in ethics, values and principles falling by the way side.[1] Media reports of various scams and financial/moral irregularities and human rights violations are but some indications of the broader decline of values and principles. The general decline of values all over is seriously affecting the moral fibre of our leaders. Ethics is a critical component of any organization's climate.

What Is Ethics?

In order to understand the nuances of ethics in the military environment perhaps it would be best to have clearly before us the definition of the issues we are addressing. For this, four words whose definition was sought from the Oxford Dictionary included 'ethics', 'integrity', 'honesty', and 'moral'. The dictionary definitions are as under:

- Ethics: Moral principles that govern a person's behavior or the conduct of an activity.
- Integrity: The quality of being honest and having strong moral principles.
- Honesty: Free of deceit, untruthfulness and sincere.
- Moral: Concerned with the principles of right and wrong behavior.

It might be noticed that none of these four definitions mention the words legal, lawful, according to rules, etc. All the four relate to a person's own principles, his respect for truth and his own innate judgment of his own conduct which keeps him on the path of right behavior. He is expected to do this, regardless of what the law says, out of his own conviction and free of the pressure of either his peers or his superiors watching him and then pulling him up for wrongful behavior. Ethics and integrity, therefore, have to come from within and cannot be superimposed. To help a person to behave ethically we have laws, codes of conduct, systems of checks and a standard of what is acceptable to society, but these by themselves cannot create morality, uprightness, honesty or ethical behavior. These have to come from within the individual.[2]

Ethics And Its Military Context

The word 'ethics' owes its origin to the Greek root word 'ethicos' which has its basis on moral character. It is a philosophic discipline that primarily seeks to distinguish between what is morally good and bad, right and wrong. It is also associated with the Greek philosophers, Plato, Socrates and Aristotle. Closer home, the Bhagavad-Gita propounded the concept of 'Dharma' or 'righteousness' or doing one's duty. *'Satyam vada, Dharmam chara'* (Speak the truth and practice dharma) is also one of the important aphorisms enunciated by the ancient gurus of India. The entire discipline of ethics in Indian epics is built on the concept of *'Dharma'*-denoting a mode of life or a code of conduct. One would also observe scriptures of all faith/ religion equally stress the need for unison of *manasa, vacha and karmana implying 'thought', 'words' and 'actions'.*

In contemporary times, ethics has come to assume two things. First, ethics refers to well based standards of right and wrong that prescribe what humans ought to do, usually in terms of rights, obligations, benefits to society, fairness, or specific virtues. Second, ethics refers to the study and development of one's ethical standards. It is necessary to constantly examine one's standards to ensure that they are reasonable and well founded. It also implies a continuous effort of studying our own moral beliefs and our moral conduct, and striving to ensure that we, and the institutions we help to shape, live up to standards that are reasonable and solidly based. The duty to set the example for others falls to the greatest degree on the most respected and qualified members of the profession, for us in the armed forces, namely, on us as officers. Professions create their own standards of performance and codes of ethics to maintain their effectiveness.

As an organized discipline, ethics emphasizes systematically finding the best reasons for making particular choices or crafting particular policies. It can be thought of as a guide to using one's freedom to choose. Military ethics applies to a specialized realm and has developed principles appropriate to it over time to help guide future practices.[3]

Military ethics being a normative discipline deals in values and how to choose among them. It does not aim to describe the world of human conduct as it is, but rather to prescribe how things ought to be, providing a road map for informing decisions and improving the reality of life. As an organized discipline, it acts as a guide in distinguishing between better and worse reasons behind a particular course of action and choosing the most reasonable path in the light of values we cherish. Military ethics is applied ethics in a leadership environment. There is nothing theoretical about it and its adequacy and legitimacy are in the individual's conscience. Leadership demands an ethical example and this is best summarized and exemplified in the well known "*Chetwode*" motto:

"The safety, honor and welfare of the country comes first, always and every time.

The honor, welfare and comfort of the men you command come next.

Your own ease, comfort and safety comes last, always and every time".[4]

These are hallowed words which reverently dictate what we as officers and leaders ought to be, what we can be, and what we will be. They are our rallying points for they mould us in uniform as custodians of our nation's defense. It is the motto that drives every officer through a demanding career, through war and peace. Whilst some may fail its acid test, to the majority it becomes a way of life, thus, ensuring that India has one of the finest and most professional armed forces in the world. It is the spirit of this credo imbibed in every officer that binds him to his men in an unshakable bond of camaraderie.

Our way of life and our well being in the Services depends upon the ability of leaders at all levels to inspire and lead often under the most harrowing conditions and unimaginable levels of stress. How do we go about these duties is important question that appears before us. The military ethos or its ethics has an important role to play here.

The military ethics is the collection of values, beliefs, ideals, principles, and other moral-ethical knowledge held by the Services and embedded in its culture. It inspires and regulates ethical individual and organizational behavior in the application of military power in defense of and service to the nation. The core of our profession is our ethic. Ethics has a special meaning to the profession of arms because it calls upon its members to make the unreserved supreme sacrifice of life at the bidding of a superior. Hence, unless a man has firm faith in the ethical correctness of the superior's motives and conduct, he will lack conviction in his act and will avoid risks to his life and honor.

This institutional ethic is derived from the imperatives of military effectiveness and values of the society the armed forces serve. Further, the Services self-polices in such a manner that leaders at all levels guard the integrity of the profession of arms inclusive of both its expertise and its ethics. They set standards for conduct and performance, teach those standards to others, establish systems that develop members to meet those standards and take rapid action against those who fail to achieve the same.

Attributes of Ethical Leadership

Leadership is 'the process of influencing others in order to gain their willing consent in the ethical pursuit of missions'. Leadership influence does not derive from positional power or authority but from character. Leaders inspire others when they are recognized as ethical people who instill trust and commitment in the pursuit of missions by ethical means. Leaders embody the ideals of the profession of arms.[5]

Researchers in the field of applied psychology define Ethical Leadership as: 'Demonstration of appropriate conduct through personal actions and relationships and the promotion of such conduct to subordinates through two-way communication, reinforcement, and decision making'.[6] Authentic, Transformational, and Ethical leadership are at the heart of our military profession. Leaders at all levels set the ethical tone for subordinates in their units and establishments either by omission or commission and have a significant impact on how their subordinates act and perform. As an officer, be it be on a staff/instructional/ command assignment, he must exhibit three important traits to create conditions for her/his unit or establishment to be successful. He must:

- Be cognizant of his part in preserving his traditional role as guarantor of Service values. He must articulate and communicate an ethical organizational vision. He must hold people accountable and put ethics above short-term interests.
- Act as ethical standard-bearer to model the ideal and to forge an atmosphere of trust and confidence. Trust has its roots in strong values and ethics that influence one's perception of situations and problems. Trust is a function of character and competence and both are vital. [7]
- Act as a teacher, to show sub-ordinates how to do what is required and to encourage them to do the same. A leader must model appropriate behavior and expectations. He must hold himself to high

ethical standards and strive for honesty, humility, and integrity in his life. As a leader he must accept responsibility for his own ethical failings.

- Communication of proper ethical standards is the foundation upon which leadership is built. While official policy may be clear and specific, if leaders by action, indicate ethical and moral behavior is not important, that perspective will prevail. Good leaders make it clear that there is no excuse for poor behavior. Commitment to our highest aspirations, openness and self-correction is the essence of ethics in military leadership.Ethical leadership requires ethical leaders. If leaders are ethical, they can ensure that ethical practices are carried out throughout the organization. It will not be necessary to define ethical leadership in words only. Instead it will be demonstrated by the leaders.

Fault Lines in Ethical Conduct Affecting Military Leadership

The nature of the military system in itself is able to breed some of the ethical dilution visible presently, the primary reason being military structure, which is extremely pyramidical and highly bureaucratic. High ambition leads to a drive for success in which ethical sensitivity is bought off or sold because of the personal need to achieve. Related to military ethic and moral values, the stated pressures manifest themselves as:

- **Loyalty Syndrome**—The problem arises when a genuine, wholesome loyalty to the boss, degenerates into covering up for him, hiding things, or not differing with him when he is wrong. Ambition is an aspect, which inspires a great degree of pseudo-loyalty. Any hint of criticism, howsoever justified, is seen as a form of disloyalty. This breeds sycophancy. Sycophancy has been rightly called as the convenient path of least resistance. A less secure leader will need pseudo-loyalty, that is, fewer ideas that threaten him, and this pseudo-loyalty is sought through fear. Suppression of truth is, thus, guaranteed. We cannot and should not tolerate unethical behavior by virtue of misplaced loyalty,

- **Obsession with Image**—Officers who have become consumed by success have often been corrupted by the idea of careerism. The quest for rank and power compromises their grasp of what is right. The military is acutely conscious of its image and, at times, goes to extreme limits to protect it. Unfortunately, today in the Services, we tend to manipulate or suppress information in the name of protecting the image of the unit, the formation and, indeed, the military itself. Whereas in the loyalty syndrome people are reluctant to tell the truth, with the image syndrome they are not even interested in it. More emphasis is on 'DASH and FLASH'. We continue to hear of commanding officers (COs) hiding information, manipulating data , and not giving truthful reports, all in the name of protecting the 'name and honor' of the organization.
- **Drive for Success**—An unhealthy drive for success at all costs is perhaps the biggest ethical challenge to the Indian military. Unfortunately, we also observe in today's environment, career advancement seems to have taken precedence over professionalism in the true sense. Command assignments are viewed, more as passport to sustain the drive towards personal career advancement. The unfortunate truth is that the balance tilts in favor of the careerist as against a genuine professional. The fall-outs

can be seen in sycophancy, one-upmanship, discouragement of dissent and free expression and the no-mistake or the 'zero-error' syndrome. There can be no more insidious and certain path to demolition of Service values than the patronage of sycophancy and the 'zero error' syndrome.

- **Authoritarianism versus Personal Example**— Leaders are often entrusted with significant formal power. The abuse of this power is authoritarianism and it is wrong. 'Serve by example' is a trait practiced today by only a handful of officers. The senior ranks are guiltiest in this regard. Perks and privileges have outgrown the sense of duty. Senior officers overuse their privileges and blatantly violate the norms of propriety. There are also some seniors who have developed a yen for 'five-star' culture and ostentation, forgetting that luxury and materialism are an anathema to the profession of arms. Astounding perks, pampering, and adulation are, sometimes, the best ways to describe the lifestyles of few of the so-called successful officers. A sense of entitlement and of having great powers, gives a feeling of being omnipotent, powerful, and important, often skewing one's judgment.
- **Majority have the feeling that unethical officers are making it to higher ranks**—This view amongst officers cannot be wished away and this very impression, right or wrong, is a cause for concern. Such officers feel that promotion itself worked and it provides vindication of the means employed. Can there still be ethical questions to ask? Promotion (symbol of success) is itself evidence of a virtue, they feel. Also it has been a uniform experience in all armies of the world that during long spells of peace, it is invariably the self-seeking, hard working, and good in 'public relations' (PR) and pliable officers

who forge ahead. There are many exemptions to this.

- **Belief of ends justifying the means**—It should be an absolute rule among military people that neither the ends justify the means nor the means justify the ends. Both ends and means must be consistent with our fundamental values. Honorable ends cannot be achieved by dishonorable means and nor do honorable means justify dishonorable or unethical ends. Under all circumstances, the end can never justify the means, however expedient it may seem at the time.
- **Selfish, promotion oriented behavior, disregard for principles, accomplishing the most trivial of missions with zero defects**—Under pressure to get ahead, such an individual is tempted to pursue advancement at the expense of others, to cut corners, to seek to win at all costs, to make things seem better than they are, to take advantage, in sum, of a myopic evaluation of performance. People will do what they are rewarded for doing. The quantification system of assessment that we follow is much more important and possibly much more visible than the quality and future consequences of the means by which they are attained.
- **Aberrations in private behavior**—There is perhaps a perception prevalent amongst many that the private conduct (sexual, social) can function on a totally different plane from the public conduct or the functioning in professional fields. This kind of perception is against the very foundation of the military system, which places profound stress on the 'whole' or complete man. There cannot be incongruence between personal and professional standards, between the private and public persona without devastating harm to

one's ability to perform professionally. It is good to remember that a leader's life is so entwined with his subordinates that every action of his is a mirror for others to emulate .Hence, there is the crying need for consistent ethical and moral standards, both at work and at home.

- **Miscellaneous disturbing trends**—These include, non-reporting of an accident or a failure, giving inflated Annual Confidential Reports (ACRs), fudging various training data like firing and Battle Physical Efficiency Test (BPET) results, connivance or knowledge of next superior commander in fudging or hiding facts. Every inaccurate or untrue report weakens the military structure, damages its efficiency, and makes the system more susceptible to subsequent and even greater falsifications and inaccuracies.

The Way Forward

Ethical Climate is the pervasive characteristic of our Services that affect how decisions are made. The health of the ethical climate is based on the perception of the soldier or the follower as to how the leadership does business and thereby constituting perception of right behavior. Highest standards of ethical climate and conduct are essential to maintain a healthy military service and attract and retain the best and most talented of each new generation of entrants in the Services.

The only way forward is to recognize the fact that ethics and values in the Services are being routinely compromised. The feeling of 'if you get away with it then it does not matter if it is right or wrong', and 'it pays to be a winner' is prevalent and may be even accepted. Skeptics may even say that there is no use of study of ethics and values as they carry little meaning in the 'heat of combat operations'. Nothing can be farther from the truth as it is only when you continuously reflect on good ethics and values, will you arrive at the correct decision in battle or under pressure.

Without being too critical of ourselves, but at the same time put into place measures, checks and balances that will ensure that the ethical code of conduct of the Services reflects what is best ,few suggestions are offered. These are only reiteration of many of the things we have learnt in our life's journey in the Services.

Leaders at all levels are personally committed, credible, and willing to take action in the values they espouse.

At all levels, those who lead, need to realize what they are doing and accept responsibility for their actions. As it is remarked, 'the fish rots from the top first' and it is the head of the fish that starts stinking first, the leaders must not only exemplify service values in their words and deeds, but also create the opportunity for everyone under their command to live them as well. Setting the example is a powerful leadership tool. The significance of a leader's position as a role model cannot be overstated. Role models help in personifying the shared values and teaching others to model the values. For junior officers, the ideal role model should be his Commanding Officer (CO). Akin to physical fitness, ethical combat fitness is a command responsibility, which is inextricably linked to operational effectiveness – we ignore it at our own peril. It is important for the leaders at all levels to foster an ethical climate by making ethical expectations clear, discussing ethical concerns, dealing with ethical risks and ensuring a reprisal free environment in their own area/ zone of influence. As leaders, the responsibility is much more, for it is not merely obeying the law but doing the best to teach and inspire and lead others to live the values that we as leaders are pledged to protect and defend.

Model the Way: Leading from the Front

Personal example is the pinnacle of all leadership qualities. In fact no aspect of leadership is more powerful than the leader's personal example. By all odds the most important aspect, is to set the example in terms of our personal and professional conduct by demonstrating commitment to the highest standards of ethical conduct and continue to make diligent efforts to live up to those standards. Communicate, in no certain terms, what your standards are and be sure they understand what you mean, and what you expect and help them appreciate how that translates into day-to- day behavior. One would only add here, 'if you want to act ethically, find an ethical boss'. Titles are as they are granted but it is your behavior and conduct that wins you respect. Seniors must model the way. As it has been rightly said, 'people may doubt what you say, but they will believe what you do'. All leaders must live and breathe the ethic. Their ethical behavior will be a guide to the subordinates instead and will further be reflected in the unit as a whole.

Clearly leading from the front is critical in the Army. Leading from the front presents different challenges at different levels. Leaders who lead from the front get critical information about what is happening on the front lines, set the example, provide clear direction to the organization and build morale and the determination to win.

Transparency in working

Information accountability will ensure a more responsive officialdom instead of one used to working in a culture of misplaced secrecy. It would certainly curb people adopting devious and questionable means to find out information which otherwise is not available. With growing demand and with the introduction of Right to Information Act (RTI

Act) one is witnessing many welcome changes even in the Services. This important aspect is an essential requirement in ensuring probity especially in matters related to defense procurement. It is imperative to encourage transparency keeping in mind the demands of security, encourage candor by free and frank discussions and accept dissent not as a sign of disloyalty. It is good to remember that a reasoned debate is better than the unspoken dissent. Fairness, transparency, and consistency are the best ways of inspiring confidence, making coteries redundant and minimizing instances of perceived injustice.

Mentoring and Counseling

It is an enduring principle of the army leadership that we mentor, coach and counsel subordinates. Senior leaders have a moral and ethical responsibility to develop subordinates while balancing both short and long term needs of the army. Grooming and mentoring is the primary task of every senior which is, unfortunately, shied away for some reason or the other.

Mentoring plays a big part in developing competent and ethically sound future leaders. It is not limited to 'high potentials' or a few favorites. Counseling is an inter-personal skill essential to effective mentoring. Effective counseling helps subordinates develop personally and professionally. Ethical leaders talk with and not to soldiers. Regular, effective counseling is essential for ethical development, and responsibility for this issue must be equally shared by the institution, its leaders and subordinates. The second-in-command of a unit could be considered for being designated as 'Unit Ethics Counselor/Coordinator'. Likewise, at the Brigade and Divisional levels, the deputy commander/ Deputy General Officer Commanding (Dy GOC) could be entrusted with similar tasks. At the Corps and Command levels, the Chief of Staff (COS) should be assigned such tasks of overseeing and keeping a watch on the ethical climate prevailing in their respective areas of responsibility. Appropriate rank/appointment holders in other two Services could be identified for such oversight.

Walk the Talk

Another cliché that means the same thing is 'Practice what you preach'. It is the opposite of being a hypocrite. It is, unfortunately, common to hear people in business and other organizations describing how they do not believe what they are being told, or how the 'management' says one thing and does another. The term 'Walking the Talk' has become an everyday phrase and with the theme of 'empowerment', people are being challenged more and more to 'model' what they say they believe. It means to be consistent with your words and actions. Today, we may all have learnt how to 'talk' to one another with all the techniques that are given in the books, but if the words are not connected to our psyche, others will find it hard to believe in what we say. Sometimes the greatest distance we have to travel, is the distance from our mouths to our feet. Military professionals can never afford to be ethically passive or lazy; they must be fully aware of what they are doing and always accept total responsibility for their actions.

Adopting Institutional Measures: Creating Right Environment by Affirming Shared Values

Systems and structures must be in place to support and reinforce its values. Ensure enforcement of ethical code by rewarding ethical behavior and disciplining non-ethical conduct. We need to reward and acknowledge ethical behavior and punish or penalize bad behavior. These actions need to be seen and projected to all. This is a powerful way to send signals about desirable and undesirable behaviors. All espoused values must be well integrated in organization's decision making process. Also we must remember that we cannot envision all of the circumstances requiring ethical decisions and choices by professional soldiers. It is, hence, essential to win trust, confidence and loyalty of increasingly discerning, aware and intelligent subordinates. The Services are value based organizations that stress the importance of the team over the individual. Values that emphasize only individual self-interest are cold comfort in times of hardship and danger. Rather, we emphasize 'Shared Values' the values that make an individual reach beyond self. The message is 'affirm shared values', for they encourage ethical behavior and foster team work and espirit-de-corps. They also promote higher levels of loyalty and foster pride about the unit/establishment and the military itself. In short, they articulate and embody the purpose and values of the organization.

Assessment of Ethical Climate

In the Services more than in any other organization, it is especially important for people to have confidence in the organization's ethical environment because much of what is necessary in war goes against the grain of the values individuals bring into the Services. Just because a leader sets a good ethical example does not mean subordinates will follow it. Some of them may feel that circumstances justify unethical behavior. Therefore, leaders must constantly pay careful attention to the team's current ethical climate and take prompt action to correct any discrepancies between it and the highest standards. It would, hence, be very good to have an assessment of the ethical climate of a unit or establishment periodically by some structured methodology. Defense Institute of Psychological Research (DIPR) could be consulted to design an appropriate assessment tool for this purpose. The assessment tool could include, among other things, identifying unit member's commitment to values, unit / work place policies and practices, unit leader's actions and environmental/mission factors. This exercise would help in taking/identifying actions necessary to accomplish this vital leader function.

A Formal and Progressive Ethical Training

Pouring abstract ethical wine into practical military bottles is no mean effort. The need to progressively stress these aspects as one progresses in one's service life would imply that we need to ensure that ethics and ethics training need to be as important as technical, tactical and physical proficiency. Ethics must be ingrained and integrated into all Services and joint training programs. Some effective methods of ethics-specific training include:

- A building block approach can be introduced wherein we need to start early and reinforce that training more frequently in an officer's career; ethics training must become an essential part of each Service's professional military education from the initial entry training to general/flag officer education. Case studies and their analyses would help the officer to understand what is right and wrong.
- Training that does not separate ethics from tactics at every level of professional military education should receive an emphasis on education and training in moral and ethical issues.
- Tactical decision games, discussion groups, vignettes, scenarios, and simulations as effective tools to be made available to leaders at all levels.
- The emphasis should be on small groups with interactive and continuous communications versus power point-dominated training.
- An "Ethics Instructor Course" could be considered for introduction by Army Training Command

(ARTRAC) at the Institute of National Integration (INI), Pune. It is also learnt that some re-designation and relocation of this institution is being contemplated.

Some specific targeted approaches could be:

- Targeting senior leadership with the philosophic and academic discussion on military ethic.
- Targeting mid-level leadership about the value of and understanding the military ethic.
- Targeting soldiers with recognizing and valuing the military ethics.

From the first moment of one's introduction to military life whether in basic training or in academies/schools of instruction/colleges of higher learning, one should never lose out the experience of a new climate that exalts and inculcates ethical propriety. At the same time we must also keep in mind that rigors of battlefield turbulence attenuate training's usefulness over a period of time and that the quality and quantity of training must be sufficient to compensate.

It is said that old dogs cannot be taught new tricks. One does not like to admit it but there may be some truth in it. Any attempt to change the ethos of the Services must involve actions at all the three levels of leadership, namely, the direct (tactical), directional (operational) and conceptual (strategic) levels. Senior officers would have to take up and accept this gauntlet to set the process going (top-down approach). At the same time, a bottom-up approach would also need to be initiated to bring about changes in officers at lower and middle levels. If we can synchronize these efforts we would have made a great beginning to set things right. Training on how to deal with situations with an ethical dimension and how to anticipate situations that involve ethical choices can go a long way towards ethical institutional practices.

However, simply injecting another block of instruction on ethics as an 'easy fix' would not solve the problem. Rather ethics and ethical behavior must be inculcated into military culture and incorporated as part of all training events. Ethics must be viewed as a way of life and an ethical foundation developed early among all military members from initial training onward. It must be reinforced by the leader's behavior 'on' and 'off' duty. The development of moral character and military competence is inextricably intertwined not only in battlefield effectiveness but also through right understanding and living out of the Services' ethics.[8]

Screening before Intake

Service Selection Boards (SSBs) and recruiting organizations are expected to screen aspirants for their beliefs in the value systems of the Services. Those found wanting should not be selected. Our present systems at the SSBs need to be updated and modernized keeping in mind the present day environment especially when the civil society is showing signs of ethical laxity. At present, we have no system for any such tests for inducting personnel below officer's ranks. DIPR must undertake this exercise with the active involvement of the three Services in designing suitable tests and checks and balances to ensure that at the induction level itself, we are able to weed out undesirable elements. There is a need to periodically assess if our selection instruments are achieving the desired purpose and suitable feedback reports are sought from the concerned Services at some specified service period. One such check could be instituted before a person is being considered for command/sensitive assignments.

Professional Ethical Code: Beyond the 'Chetwode' Motto

Beyond the ends of wartime efficacy and retention of public trust, the Army needs an institutional ethic to safeguard its profession. Scattered exhortations exist but it would add strength to their application if they were founded in formality. Here, it is not the intention to question the relevance of the inspiring beacon of the '*Chetwode*' motto, but the concern often expressed is that the ethical standards taught to the cadets do not serve them well, when they move into leadership positions in the 'real world' of the armed forces. When new officers leave their basic schools and training centers and enter the Army at large, they have major adjustments to make. A young warrior, as he can be rightly called is loud, proud and motivated after his pre-commission training and then becomes disillusioned on arrival at his first unit. This situation could be caused by lax standards, poor unit work ethic and discipline, hypocrisy by leaders, too little hands-on training and too little leader mentoring. Things are different and radically so, in the larger world, where practice takes over from theory. Many hold the view that the '*Chetwode*' motto though a very reasonable and practical guide to professional behavior especially when you are in direct contact with troops, is an *insufficient guide* as it becomes less influencing as one moves away from direct (tactical) to organizational (operational) to strategic levels of leadership. In other words, they are all right but it is not enough.

It is suggested that we should try to work out for ourselves a code of conduct that might help us to cope with our ethical problems—one which we would consider worthy of adoption by the entire officer cadre. Professional military ethic must be functional, i.e.; it must accommodate the features necessary for effective performance in battle. Obviously, the ethic must be legal, and must conform to all established laws. And perhaps less obviously but no less important, the ethic must be culturally and politically acceptable, i.e., it must conform to the dictates of our national values. The product thus formed is a complex pattern of normative practices expressible in terms of principles. It should be inspirational, philosophically defensible, persuasive and an exhortation to better behavior, rather than a list of do's and don'ts. So, for an expression of our ethic to be functional it must also be fairly comprehensive. In a profession as diverse as ours (ranging from young, minimally educated enlisted personnel to highly educated senior officers), this is no small challenge. Ideally, the code should supply a moral direction to know what is right and inspire moral commitment in advance and to motivate members to act in accordance with their knowledge.

Spiritual Influence/Fitness: A Key Component

Spirituality is a discipline that has been generally mistaken for religion. Spirituality represents the essence of religion. While religion has rituals, spirituality focuses on principles, values and ethics, passions, meaning, clarity, direction, authenticity, purpose and presence. These aspects are enhanced when leaders tap into their deeper selves.

The necessity of spiritual support for personnel in crisis has been recognized not only in the Services, but also by civilian law enforcement and disaster relief personnel. Spiritual fitness in the Services means the ability of the individual to believe in the importance, necessity, and just nature of the mission; to have faith in the reliability of leaders; in the dependability of his fellow comrades; and in the training and equipment furnished for the operation; and to be prepared to encounter and cope with extreme danger, devastation, and even death with confidence, dedication, and courage.[9]

Spiritual fitness transcends moral fitness because it

prepares the individual to deal with ultimate questions such as the meaning of life and not merely questions of proper behavior. Spiritual strength for many is supported by their religious convictions; for others who may not be religious, it may be an expression of their loyalty to the nation, to the unit and to their fellow comrades. Spiritual strength is an inspirational trait which can motivate a unit even when circumstances are bleak. There is an aspect of courage which comes from a deep spiritual faith which when prevalent in a unit, can result in uncommon toughness and tenacity in combat. We must be diligent in strengthening the moral and spiritual fitness of our personnel. Spiritual fitness reinforces such values as respect for others, loyalty, and selfless service.

Practice of Meditation

As a suggestion at an individual level, the practicing of meditation as means of self-introspection is being recommended. We are all aware that there are many schools of meditation that are being talked about, but all of them help a person to take that inward journey to look within himself. Meditation trains our mind to regulate itself, leads us beyond the outer activity into the inner silence of our hearts. Here we find ourselves connected to our Divine essence or by whatever name one may like to call it.

The regulated mind and connection with our inner self develops in us a balanced state which is unaffected by the ups and downs of everyday life. Our natural capacity for wisdom and right action begins to manifest, allowing us to prioritize the conflicting demands of life. Sustained practice of meditation develops a constant balanced state, a deep sense of connection with our inner selves and a lasting direction and meaning to our lives.[10]

More and more people around the globe are turning to meditation, realizing that in order to reach our full potential as complete, balanced human beings; our inner spiritual longings must be addressed along with the material demands of daily life. It helps to detach ourselves from useless aspects, from superfluous things, diverting ourselves from the harshness of certain images, of sounds increasingly louder in terms of decibels. By the practice of meditation we refine our perceptions, improve our inner poise and get transformed little by little. We develop a sense of detachment and reflective intelligence and, thus, are able to control, modify and overcome the force of our gregarious instincts and frenzied individualism throwing up the best and worst in us. There is no spiritual search without a reappraisal and intensive work on oneself.

It is worth considering that along with Yoga which is being encouraged in the academies, some exposure to 'meditation' techniques could be institutionalized. Recent workshops conducted under the aegis of Army Training Command (ARTRAC) at the Officers Training Academy (OTA), National Defence Academy (NDA) and Indian Military Academy (IMA) has been very well received by the cadets.

Conclusion

Our Services are framed by our preparedness to bear personal and collective risk, and by our resolve to apply force wherever and whenever this is necessary. Leadership in the Services is based upon the premise that for the Services to contribute to the defense of our country and its national interests, it is necessary not only to maintain an operationally capable force but also an ethically dependable force: one which abides both by the letter and by the spirit of the laws of armed conflict. For the Services to be ethically dependable in this way, it must be ethically led at all levels.

Leaders inspire others when they are recognized as ethical people who energize trust and commitment in the pursuit of missions by ethical means. Leaders embody the ideals of the profession of arms. Leadership amplifies command and leaders bring strength of character to command positions. Leaders model professional ideals, reinforce Services' values and enrich positions of command with moral insight. Ethical leadership entails creating ethical command climates that set the conditions for positive outcomes and ethical behavior.[11] We have more control over the professional environment than we may realize. A sense of moral resilience is what all leaders need in order to address the pressing challenges that we face now and in the years ahead.

No one could possibly argue that adherence to ethical standards and the responsibility to leaven the officer corps in terms of its ethical norms is free of risk or even easy. It is just essential. It is simple as all that. Doing right ourselves, teaching what is right to our troops, and encouraging all others with whom we come in contact (including peers and seniors) to do what is right—that is what we are training officers to do, what the Services needs them to do and what the nation relies on them tó do. On this everything else depends. Ethics are never dispensable as they form an integral part of human survival. Standing firm ethically can exact a cost, perhaps a steep one. As professionals we must be willing to pay it.

References

1. Subramaniam, Arjun, 'Ethics and Values in Military Leadership', *Air Power Journal*, Vol. 3, No. 2, April–June 2006, pp. 157-76.
2. Buch, M.N., 'Integrity and Ethics in the Civil Service', available at http://www.vifindia.org/articles/2012/december/04/integrity-and-ethics-in-the-civil-service.
3. Rhodes, Bill, *An Introduction to Military Ethics,*

Westport: Praeger Security International, 2009, pp. 2–3, available at www.abc-clio.com.

4. Field Marshal Sir Philip Chetwode, Commander-in-Chief Indian Army, 1931–32.
5. 'Leadership in the Australian Defence Forces', Canberra, ADDP00.6, Para1.8, 2006, available at http://www.cda-acd.forces.gc.ca
6. Barnes, Christopher M. and Joseph Doty, 'What Does Contemporary Science Say about Ethical Leadership?', *Military Review*, Vol. 90, No. 5, September–October 2010, pp. 90-93.
7. Covey, Stephen M.R., *The Speed of Trust – The One Thing that Changes Everything*, New York: Free Press, 2006, pp. 30–31.
8. Snider, Don M., 'Moral Corrosion within our Military Professionals', 27 November 2012, available at http://strategicstudyindia.blogspot.in/2012/11/the-moral-corrosion-within-our-military.html
9. Brinsfield, John W., 'Army Values and Ethics: A Search for Consistency and Relevance', *Parameters*, Vol. 28, No. 3, Autumn 1998, pp. 69–84.
10. Available at http://en.wikipedia.org/wiki/Meditation, accessed on 30 January 2013.
11. ARTRAC, *Manual on Command*, 2012.

2

The Moral Dimensions of Transformational Leadership*

"Transformational leaders choose the path of courage to be and do what is right and best rather than choosing the easy and expedient"

Rob Inrig in "Leading from Your Strengths"

(* Published in 'The War College Journal' ,Volume 42,Winter 2013, pp 26-29)

Introduction

Probably as long ago as our cave dwelling days, human beings have been concerned with the ethics of our leaders. Our history books are replete with description of good and bad kings, great and evil empires, and strong and weak men at the helm of affairs of the state. We too have our epics–

both Ramayana and Mahabharata offering a good insight into the moral dimensions of leadership. No study of Indian culture can avoid the interpretations of these two great epics. A significant portion of these epics deal with moral dilemmas. These moral dilemmas are universal in the sense that they mostly represent a conflict in the state of mind and are found in everyday life. They are like logical paradoxes which cannot be easily solved. Various methods resolution or dissolution of moral dilemmas can be delineated in the epics. It is quite extraordinary how the word *DHARMA*, an idea from the ancient Rig Veda has evolved and enriched itself over three thousand years through a process of contestation and adaptation.[1] Both Lord Rama and Lord Krishna seem to hold deontological point of view. [2]

"Karmanye Vadhikaraste, Ma Phaleshou Kada Chana"

(To work alone, you have the right, but never claim its results—Chapter2, Verse 47 of **Bhagavad Gita**)

From the perspective of Western tradition, the development of ethical theory dates back to Plato (427-347 B.C) and Aristotle (384-32 B.C). The word ethics has its roots in Greek word 'ethicos' which translates to customs, conduct, or character. Ethics is concerned with the kinds of values and morals an individual or society finds suitable or appropriate. Furthermore, ethics relates to the virtuousness of individuals and their motives. Ethical theory provides a system of rules or principles that guides us in making decisions about what is right or wrong and good or bad in a particular situation. It provides for understanding what it means to be a morally decent being.

Is Leadership a Moral Activity?

Is leadership a moral activity? This is one of the single-most important questions in the current debate about leadership. Sadly many corporate, political and military leaders seek to divorce their tasks from morality, arguing that their sole responsibility is to find effective, pragmatic solutions to problems. This is a narrow and ultimately self-defeating definition of their roles. Like much of applied philosophy, military ethics rests somewhat uneasily on a complex array of ambiguities and tensions. This is due, in part to the nature of the challenges that face the military and in part to the term 'ethics' which means different things to different people. Leadership is 'the process of influencing others in order to gain their willing consent in the ethical pursuit of missions'. Leadership influence does not derive from positional power or authority but from character. Leaders inspire others when they are recognized as ethical people who energize trust and commitment in the pursuit of missions by ethical means. Leadership demands character. Leadership defined by character and ethical purpose, co-opts and attracts others to follow willingly in response to shared ideals.

It is important to understand that ethics is a normative discipline. It deals in values and how to choose among them. It aims to describe the world of human conduct as it is, to prescribe how things ought to be, providing a road map for informing decisions and improving the reality of life. Ethics, by nature, is about aspirations of humanity at both individual and communal levels. If 'Life is what you make it', studying ethics helps provide the blue print. Ethicists acknowledge that humans and their institutions are flawed but they also suppose that they can improve if decisions follow careful ethical analysis. Indeed, if it was not for recognition of those flaws, there would be little point in worrying over ethics.[3]

An imperfect world does not constitute a reason to ignore ethics. Particularly in discussions of war, some are prone to dismissing ethics as irrelevant. 'This is war' they will say, and (quoting General Sherman) 'War is hell'. But the fact that people treat one another badly in war tells us absolutely nothing about whether they ought to do so. The fact that unethical behavior goes on and is likely to continue does not count against the study of ethics any more than the fact that terminal illness suggests the study of medicine is pointless. On the contrary, the facts of suffering and evil make the study of ethics all the more worthwhile.[4] The military profession bears an unlimited moral liability which allows no room for ethical passivity. Professional service entails constant ethical challenge, particularly with regards to human life, which must never be risked or taken without proper regard.

Ethics –The Heart of Leadership

It is a well acknowledged fact that without continuous commitment, enforcement and modeling of leadership, standards of ethics cannot be and will not be achieved in any organization. The ethics of leadership, whether they are good or bad, positive or negative, affect the ethos of the work place, and, thereby, help to form the ethical choices and decisions of the participants/members of any work force. Leaders help to set the tone, develop the vision and shape the behavior of all those involved in the organizational life. Aristotle suggested that morality cannot be learned simply by reading a treatise on virtue. The spirit of morality, said Aristotle, is awakened in the individual only through the witness and conduct of a moral person. The principle of the 'witness of another', or what we now refer to as 'patterning', 'role modeling', and 'mentoring' is predicated on a four step process, three of which follow:

- As communal creatures, we learn to conduct ourselves primarily through the actions of significant others.
- When the behaviors of others are repeated often enough to be peer-group positive, we emulate these actions.

- If and when our actions are in turn reinforced by others, they become acquired characteristics or behavioral habits.

Modeling, emulation, habit, results whether positive or negative, are neither the sufficient nor the final goal. The fourth and final step in the process must include reflection, evaluation, choice and conscious intent on the part of the actor because ethics is always "an inside-out proposition" involving free will.[5]

Essence of Transformational Leadership-Linkage to Ethics and Morals

One of the current and most popular approaches to leadership that has been the focus of much research since the early 1980s is the transformational approach. Transformational leadership's popularity might be due to its emphasis on intrinsic motivation and follower development which fits the needs of today's work environment and workforce who want to be inspired and empowered to succeed in times of uncertainty. As the name implies, Transformational leadership is a process that changes and transforms people. It is concerned with emotions, values, ethics, standards and long term goaled. It includes among other things assessing follower's motives, satisfying their needs and treating them as full human beings. Transformational leadership involves an exceptional form of influence that moves followers to accomplish more than what is usually expected of them. It is a process that often incorporates charismatic and visionary leadership. People who exhibit transformational leadership often have a strong set of internal values and ideals, and they are effective at motivating followers to act in ways that support the greater good rather than their own self interests.

One of the factors of transformational leadership is 'Idealized Influence'. It is the emotional component of leadership. These leaders act as strong role models for the followers; followers identify with these leaders and want very much to emulate them. These leaders usually have very high standards of moral and ethical conduct and can be counted on to do the right thing. They are deeply respected by followers, who usually have a great deal of trust in them. Leaders provide subordinates with a vision and a sense of mission. Transformational leadership places a strong emphasis on followers' needs, values and morals and involves attempts by leaders to move people to higher standards of moral responsibility. It includes motivating followers to transcend their own self-interests for the good of the team, organization, or community. It is fundamentally and morally uplifting. This emphasis sets the transformational approach apart from all other approaches to leadership because it suggests that leadership has a moral dimension. James MacGregor Burns acknowledged as an authority on leadership styles and who has written extensively on Transformation leadership has this to say about the linkage such a leadership style has with ethics and morals-

> *" When one or more persons engage with others in such a way that leaders and followers raise one another to higher levels of motivation and morality...Power bases are linked not as counter weights, but as mutual support for a common purpose. Transforming Leadership ultimately becomes moral in that it raises the level of human conduct and ethical aspirations of both the leaders and led and thus it has a transforming effect on both."*

Burns has defined 'moral leadership' as 'relationship... of mutual needs, aspirations and values of ...' Moral leadership emerges from, and returns to, the fundamental wants and needs, aspirations and values of the followers'.[6] Leaders are truly transformational when they increase awareness of what is right, good, important and beautiful; when they foster in followers higher moral authority; and when they move followers to go beyond their self-interests for the good of their group, organization or society. For Burns, transformational leadership is motivating, uplifting and ultimately 'moral' in that it raises the level of human conduct and ethical aspiration of both the leader and the led.

Summarizing briefly the principles, practices and values of Transformational leadership it can be said to include the following: [7]

- Stress on Human development.
- Trust is the variable intervening Transformational leadership and its outcomes.
- Individualized consideration.
- Alignment of individual and organizational goals.
- Inspirational motivation/Intellectual stimulation.
- Authenticity. Resolves values-conflicts.

Conclusion

In the study of ethics and leadership, ethical theories can be thought of as falling within two broad domains: theories about leaders' conduct and theories about leaders' character. Stated another way, ethical theories when applied to leadership are about both the actions of leaders and who they are as people. Burns' theory of transformational leadership views it as morally uplifting process. It is unique in that it makes ethics the central characteristic of the leadership process. Steven Covey the author of many books especially on leadership very aptly sums up what it all means. *"The goal of transformational leadership is to 'transform' people and organizations in a literal sense – to change them in mind and heart; enlarge vision, insight, and understanding; clarify purposes; make behavior congruent with beliefs, principles, or values; and bring about changes that are permanent, self-perpetuating, and momentum building."* Here in this quote one can discern a special message that is being conveyed in the above definition in that 'Leadership is a relationship', a relationship between those who aspire to lead and those who choose to follow. It is the quality of this relationship, a relationship characterized by mutual respect and confidence that will overcome the greatest adversities and leave a legacy of excellence and brilliance.[8]

Need of truly transformational leaders is to promote within their organization, ethical policies, procedures, and processes. They need to be committed to a clearly stated, continually enforced code of ethical conduct that helps establish acceptable ethical standards. They need to foster an organizational culture with high ethical standards. If this is done correctly, transformational leadership can stand as a beacon for those interested in the pursuit of ethical leadership.

References

1. Gurcharan Das, '*The Difficulty of Being Good*', Penguin Books, p311.
2. K.C. Pandey, '*Ethics and Epics: Reflections on Indian Ethos*', Read worthy, New Delhi, p 1
3. Bill Rhodes, '*An Introduction to Military Ethics.*' Praeger Security International, p 3.
4. ibid.
5. Stephen R.Covey '*The Seven Habits of Highly Effective People* (New York: A Fireside Book, 1990), pp 42, 43.
6. James MacGregor Burns, '*Leadership*' (New York: Harper and Row, 1978), p 4
7. Bernard Bass, 'The Ethics of Transformational Leadership' in '*Ethics-The Heart of Leadership*' edited

by Joanne B.Ciulla, p179.

8. Extracts from a paper presented by the author on "Relevance of Ethical Leadership in the Process of Transformation" at a Panel discussion on "Transformational Leadership in Changing Times" held at College of Defence Management, Secunderabad (AP) in 2010.

3

Role of Leadership in Ethical Climate Building

"...by establishing norms...of ethical behavior, organizations influence the moral reasoning of the individual, causing them to act as...those around them do. It is important to also note that leaders may play a paramount role in setting the ethical climate of an organization."

K. Kelloway, *Literature Review: Towards a Model of Ethical Decision Making in Organizations* (Ottawa: DHRRE Publications, 1999).

Introduction

Victor and Cullen (1988 cited by Cohen 1993, p.344) defined ethical climate as the persistent moral atmosphere of a social system, characterized by mutual perceptions of right and wrong, as well as common assumptions about how moral concerns should be addressed.[1] Ethical climate is best understood as part of an organization's culture, and how it responds to ethical issues. Ethical climate determines what members believe is right or wrong and shapes their ethical decision making and behavior. Leaders are responsible for creating the organization we admire for their ethical behavior. They are in fact the 'ethics officers' of their organization and followers look to them as role models and act accordingly. They are generally seen as legitimate, credible, and attractive because they occupy positions of authority. Leaders increase legitimacy by treating their subordinates and followers fairly and boost their attractiveness by expressing care and concern.[2]

Leadership is the single most important variable impacting unit ethical climate. Examples of failed cases demonstrate the criticality of leaders' role and the significant consequences of not understanding that role. Military leaders are the moral arbiters in war.[3] They serve as values champions and are responsible for the ethical climate of their units. The laws of war and rules of engagement serve as their guideposts. The degree to which a unit complies with the rules and conventions that constrain combat operations serves as an indication of its ethical climate. Organizations with stronger ethical climates have less severe ethical problems, and are more successful at resolving such issues should they arise.[4]

Shaping Ethical Contexts

Management professors Bart Victor and John Cullen are of the view that ethical climates can be broadly classified according to the criteria members use to make moral choices and the group's members refer to, when making ethical determinations.[5] Five primary ethical climates identified by them include:

- **Instrumental:** It follows the principle of 'ethical egotism'. Such people make decisions based on selfish interests that serve the individual.

- **Caring:** It emphasizes concern or care for others.
- **Law and Order:** Such a climate is driven by external criteria such as professional codes of conduct.
- **Rules:** Such a climate is governed by the policies, rules, and procedures developed in the organization.
- **Independence:** Such a climate gives members wide latitude to make their own decisions.

Leaders would do well to discern the particular ethical orientation of their organization as each of these five types of climates poses unique ethical challenges. Members are most satisfied when their personal ethical preferences match those of their organization.

Signs Of a Positive And Healthy Ethical Climate

A positive and healthy ethical ambience will be visible by:

- Zero Tolerance for destructive behaviors characterized by incivility, aggression, sexual/ gender harassment, and discrimination.
- Integrity, displaying ethical soundness, wholeness, and consistency.
- Concern for means and ends.
- Fair and transparent reward systems.
- Unbiased performance and evaluation processes.
- Clearly spelt-out decision making rights and responsibilities

Indicators for Positive Ethical Climate

In a positive ethical climate, the immediate superior will :

- Insist and enforce high ethical standards.
- Be effective in demonstrating core values.
- Be effective in setting standards for integrity.
- Interact with model good ethical behavior.
- Lead by example and 'Up from the Front'.
- Transparent in ethical decision making process.
- Conduct an 'After Action Session/Report' following an ethical issue.

Causes of Negative and Indifferent Ethical Climate

Over many occasions in the past few months, media accounts have highlighted instances pointing to the erosion of values in the Services. The feeling of 'if you get away with it, then it does not matter if it is right or wrong' and 'it pays to be a winner' is widely prevalent and may be even accepted. Skeptics may even say that there is no use of study of ethics and values as they carry little meaning in the 'heat of combat operations'. Nothing can be farther from the truth as it is only when you continuously reflect on good ethics and values will you arrive at the correct decision in battle or under pressure.

Recent events illustrate that unethical conduct that violates the laws of war occur with unfortunate regularity, even in the well trained and professional Indian Army and other security forces. While some might argue that the scope of such misconduct is not extensive in a force of over a million, the issue is not whether it is happening in two percent or twenty percent of our units, but it is still very disturbing. Even if one accepts that laws of war transgressions are relatively infrequent, the negative impact is significant. The frequency of incidents only suggests that we should be doing all we can to ensure all our units have the right ethical climate.

It is common knowledge that in today's information age, the tactical actions of small units and individuals can have strategic impact. This impact can be positive or negative but is rarely neutral. The strategic impact of unethical acts challenges our ability to maintain the moral high ground, reduces public support and plays into our opponent's propaganda machine. These acts are detrimental to the military's ability to achieve assigned strategic objectives and they lead directly to the second matter of importance. Unethical acts are detrimental to the military's professional stature, domestically, internationally, and within the profession itself. Military stature matters because it is related to the degree to which the military is deemed acceptable as a viable element of national power.[6]

Acceptability is one of the litmus tests used to evaluate strategic options. Unethical acts also have significant short and long term impact on our soldiers' welfare. This is true in at least two respects. Firstly at the most basic level, soldiers will be held accountable for unethical acts that violate the laws of war. Aside from the legal argument, soldiers have to live with the psychological and emotional impact of their actions. Secondly, unethical behavior destroys trust, morale, and cohesion.[7] If we either let soldiers intentionally conduct unethical acts, or if we intentionally have them conduct unethical acts, we are then failing to 'take care of soldiers' in the true professional sense.

The nature of complex counter-insurgency (CI) operations makes ethical decision making and application of laws of war extremely difficult. In these operations the lines between peace and war, combatants and non-combatants, and degrees of proportionality are more blurred and fluid than ever. Proportionality implies the effort to minimize the harm done to non-combatants against war aim of accomplishing the military objectives. This factor makes it difficult for soldiers to make the best ethical choices. The stress of extended combat also has a deleterious effect on soldiers' and leaders' decision making.

The Role of the Commander/Leader

The commander/leader (at any level) is the single most important factor in creating a climate that produces ethical behavior evidenced by the adherence to the laws of war and rules of engagement. They enhance credibility by living the values they espouse. Their mere presence acts as a moral influence agent ensuring that ethics messages are not drowned out by other messages about tasks and missions.

This in turn suggests that the commander/leader is a determining factor in the ethical behavior of units. Nature of command makes command climate an important variable in ethical behavior of soldiers and units. Understanding these aspects and how they are related illuminates why this is true. We first need to consider the commander's/leader's responsibility to understand and translate the military ethic (culture) to specific conditions so his unit can apply it. First, it means that 'they are responsible for everything their command does or fails to do' and second, it implies 'Commanders and other army leaders committed to the professional army ethic promote a positive environment'. These concepts of responsibility for action and promoting an ethic explicitly state that a commander's/leader's duty to insure his soldiers' translation of the laws of war to any given situation is commensurate with his own.

In organizations like the military, the least experienced members of the organization (soldiers) are the executors of policy.[8] Also, as highlighted earlier, the complex and decentralized nature of today's military operations make application of the laws of war difficult. For these reasons, the commander/leader who have internalized the military ethic (through time, education and experience) must understand and translate the laws to the specific conditions for the benefit of less experienced soldiers. The degree to which the commander/leader does this well will have a large impact on his unit's ethical performance. Good commanders/leaders will establish an appropriate ethical stance; bad commanders will reveal their ignorance.[9] It is imperative that the commander/leader add clarity for soldiers in ambiguous conditions. The commander's/ leader's understanding of and ability to translate just war theory and the laws of war will significantly impact the ethical climate he develops.

What a Leader/Commander cannot be is: [10]

- An Unethical leader who falls short both as a moral person and a moral influence agent and communicates that ethics don't matter and just only results are his concern.
- A hypocritical leader who just talks about values, but doesn't live up to the rhetoric.
- An ethically neutral leader who is not clearly seen as neither ethical or un-ethical as he does not send out strong messages about ethics and leaves followers unsure; a leader who gives an impression of being self-centered and focused on bottom-line.

Recognizing and Fostering an Ethical Command Climate

While it is beyond the scope of this paper to detail a comprehensive list of characteristics of a positive command climate that fosters ethical behavior, a few key points are worth consideration. An underlying aspect of positive climate is command presence. Commanders cannot assume that subordinate leaders are steeped in the military ethic and laws of war logic. They cannot know how their subordinates are applying it, if they are not out among them.

Presence also creates a building block for trust as it is paramount to good command climates. Trust is also the portal to the developmental process as it allows for candid non-attribution after action reviews that can be used to teach, coach, and mentor not just an individual but the entire unit. Tied to the notion of trust is the necessity of insuring there is no 'zero defect' mentality in the unit. A 'zero defect' mentality runs counter to the developmental process because it implies the leaders' role is not to coach and mentor. Presence, trust, and a tolerant environment are fundamental to creating a climate that fosters development, continuous improvement, and growth.[11]

To ensure units have positive command climates that foster ethical behavior, the Services need to make sure that commanders are not sacrificing investment in the growth and development of the unit, leaders, and soldiers, for the sake of the immediate mission. By balancing these two aspects of command responsibility, commanders will actually improve performance of the immediate mission in the future.[12] By focusing attention on ethics with frequent communication about values, mission, military ethos, and importance of ethical standards, one can discern a qualitative improvement of the ethical climate.

Ethical Climate Building Tools[13]

To create ethical organizational climates, leaders can employ following three tools :

- Core values of the organization.
- Guiding ethical code well arrived at and communicated.
- Ethical learning/training.

Core Values of the Organization

Identifying and applying the ethical core values is an important step to create a highly moral climate. They unite any establishment around its purpose and vision. The congruence of our stated values and our actual practices is pivotal to any organization's success. The Services are a value-based organization that stresses the importance of the team over the individual. Shared values make an individual reach beyond self. Core values build strong cohesive organizations that, in turn, become the source of strength and solidarity for their members in difficult and turbulent times. Value- based leadership means setting the example and then creating a command culture where soldiers can put values into practice. It is leadership best described by a simple principle of 'What leader should *Be*, What he should *Know*, What he should *Do*, and What he should *Achieve*'.

Guiding Ethical Code Well Arrived at and Communicated

Codes of ethics are among the most common ethic tools. Can a written code of ethics curtail, if not curb ethical abuse? Skeptics make comments such as that they are too vague to be useful, are developed as public relations documents designed to improve an organizations image, and often lack adequate enforcement provisions. Increasingly, Medicine and Law are not only thinking about how to assure that professionals are morally sensitive but also how to educate them in identifying and resolving ethical issues that come up in professional-client relationships. Very often in the search of an ethical code, at least in the Army, one falls back on the famous '*Chetwode' motto*'- the hallowed words which reverently dictate what we as officers and leaders *ought to be*, we can be, and what we should be. Despite disparities between these precepts and the practices observable within the officer corps, this motto still provides a useful and workable ideal for the motivation and guidance of the military professional.

A 'perfect code' may be misleading for in real life it may turn out to be different. What is important is that the code must allow each person to address personally important issues at a particular moment in their life. The code represents a journey of personal reflection, a journey necessary for skillful ethical decision making. We must acknowledge here that many times, the real world issues are tough to describe accurately let alone address successfully. The best we can do is to do our best. Adherence to codes should be acknowledged and rewarded where possible.

Ethical Learning and Training

Organizations must be concerned about continuous ethical improvement or what may be referred to as 'Total Ethical Improvement (TEI) something similar to Total Quality Management (TQM) which is a buzz word at many corporate entities. Factors that should encourage ongoing ethical learning will include:

- **Risk Assessments:** As has been seen from the recent cases of ethical impropriety, such happenings have even questioned the very survival of an organization. No type of organization be it a, religious, humanitarian, business, government, or military is exempt from ethical failure.
- **Ethical Weakness:** It is a truism that no organization can ever claim to have arrived when it comes to ethical development. There will always be a room for improvement. It is also seen that some of the inconsistencies observed in leaders of the organization are found in the climate of entire organization.
- **Change:** It must be recognized that each change, in turn, brings new ethical challenges. Like the environments in which we live, organizations

themselves are in a constant process of transformation. Each change alters the ethical landscape.

The ultimate task of education in ethics is to help an officer to think through his ethical codes and standards and to know what matters. Taking courses in ethics is no more a guarantee of ethical purity than teaching them. Knowledge of the good is not enough: some of us might insist upon moral courage and grace as well. However, we can be certain of one thing: having discussed, read, and written about what one ought to do, will very likely increase the chances that one will do, what one ought to do. Training on how to deal with situations with an ethical dimension, and how to anticipate situations that involve ethical choices, can go a long way toward ethical institutional practices.

The structure of an ethical environment as depicted in the Figure-1, explains all the contributory factors that foster a healthy ethical climate.

Figure-1, Structure of an Ethical Environment

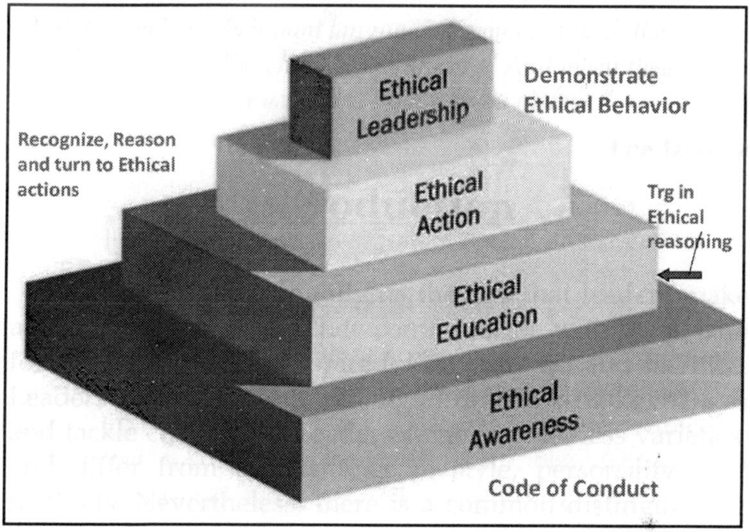

Conclusion

The officer class is increasingly veering towards careerism and material benefits. This cannot possibly be avoided given the present national, financial, and modern trends. But care needs to be taken that it not at the cost of and to the detriment of professionalism, dedication and concern for men. An ever widening chasm exists between the senior and junior echelons, because of the distancing from the ethical highway and the culture of examples being set at the highest levels. High star culture increases the chasm and breeds sycophancy. Professional efficiency and uprightness have gradually lost ground to sycophancy and a no-mistake syndrome.[14] The strength and practice of the ethos of setting an example (topmost downwards) is visibly diluted and openly talked about by junior echelons. Our penchant for exaggeration of even minor achievements and sweeping weaknesses under the carpet need to be curbed, and the high star culture and sycophancy need to be dealt with firmly.

Most men are inherently neither good nor evil. Each has within himself the capacity for actions that are admirable or reprehensible. What brings out the best or worst in us is, often, the organizational climate in which we find ourselves. In the Services there are units/establishments, which at particular times and under particular commanders, come close to living up to the ideal standards. There are others which fall lamentably short. Command climate is the commander's most powerful tool in ensuring ethical behavior. It is for this reason that leadership is the decisive factor in the shaping and building of positive ethical climate of any organization.

References

1. *Journal of Business Ethics*, Springer 2010, "Establishing

Organization Ethical Climate: How do Managerial Practices Work"?

2. "*Creating an Ethical Organizational Climate*" –Sage Publications, available at www.sagepub.com/upm-data/23172_Chapter 9.
3. Roger H Nye, *The Challenge of Command* (Wayne, NJ: Avery Publishing Group, 1986),pp 99-113.
4. L.K. Bartles, et al., "The Relationship Between Ethical Climate and Ethical Problems within Human Resource Management," *Journal of Business Ethics* 17 (1998): pp 799 – 804.
5. Victor,B & Cullen,J.B (1988). 'The organizational bases of ethical work climates', *Administrative Science Quarterly*, 33, pp 101-125.
6. Martin L. Cook, *The Moral Warrior: Ethics and Service in the US Military* (Albany, NY: State University of New York Press, 2004), pp 21- 25.
7. U.S. Department of the Army, *Army Leadership*, Field Manual 22 – 100 (Washington, DC: Department of the Army, August 1999), pg E3.
8. Michael Lipsky, *Street Level Bureaucracy* (New York: The Russell Sage Foundation, 1980), pg 4.
9. Roger H Nye, *The Challenge of Command* (Wayne, NJ: Avery Publishing Group, 1986),pp 84-90.
10. Trevino, Hartman& Brown; Trion, I.K &Nelson, K.A. (2004), '*Managing Business Ethics: Straight Talk about how to do it Right*' 3rd Edition, Chapter 9.
11. Raymond C. Hartjen Jr., *Ethics in Organizational Leadership*, Strategy Research Project (Carlisle Barracks, PA: US Army War College, May 1984), pp 79 - 80.
12. Lt Col David M. Miller, United States Army- "Leadership: the Decisive factor in the Ethical

performance of units"- USAWC Strategy Research Project, March 2006.

13. *Creating an Ethical Organizational Climate"* —Sage Publications, available at www.sagepub.com/ upm-data/23172_Chapter 9.
14. Lt Gen SC Sardeshpande (retd) – "Soldiering-An Indian Experience" by Military Affairs Series, pg 113.

4

Leadership-Ethic of Being

"Leadership is a potent combination of strategy and character. If you must be without one, be without strategy."

General H. Norman Schwarzkopf-US Army, Retired

Introduction

The word 'ethics' originated from the Latin word '*ethicus*' and the Greek word '*ethicos*' which means character or manners. The horizon of this definition may be further expanded if the concepts of right or wrong behavior or conduct are incorporated. As ethics acts as a guide of action, it can also be termed as a normative discipline. We are social creatures. More often than we realize, we get our cues for acceptable and unacceptable behavior from our environment as well as our intrinsic traits of character. This is even truer in the intense social environment of a military organization or institution. Various ethical theories provide a system of rules or principles that guide us in making decisions about what is right or wrong and good or bad in a particular situation. It provides a basis for understanding what it means to be a morally decent human being. Stated another way, ethical theories when applied to leadership are about both the actions of leaders and who they are as people.

The ethical climate of an organization or command is deeper than officially stated values and policies. Leaders are vital in creating, sustaining, and correcting that climate. No matter what they say, being perceived as fair, respectful, and straightforward, sends the most powerful message about what leaders' value and expect from the organizations they lead. When there is a breakdown in values, the military gives the commander unique tools to restore the standard, whether through formal disciplinary actions or 'all-hands' calls. The choices leaders make and how they respond in a given circumstance are informed and directed by their ethics.

Military Ethics –What Does it Mean?

Our way of life and our well being in the Services depends upon the ability of leaders at all levels to inspire and lead often under the most harrowing conditions and unimaginable levels of stress. The Military ethos or its ethics has an important role to play here. The military officer is considered a gentleman, not because nation wills it, not because it has been the custom of people in all times to afford him that courtesy, but specifically because nothing less than a gentleman is truly suited for his particular set of responsibilities.

Military ethics applies to a specialized realm and has developed principles appropriate to it over time to help guide future practices. Military ethics is a species of the genus 'professional ethics'. That is to say, it exists to be of service to professionals who are not themselves specialists in ethics but who have to carry out the tasks entrusted to the profession as honorably and correctly as possible. It is analogous to medical ethics or legal ethics in the sense that its core function is to assist those professions to think through the moral challenges and dilemmas inherent in their professional activity and, by helping members of the profession better understand the ethical demands upon them, to enable and motivate them to act appropriately in the discharge of their professional obligations.[1]

Military ethics is at its core, practical and professional. It is meant to be the handmaid of the profession of arms. It exists to assist thoughtful professionals to think through their real-world problems and issues. Although there are few conceptual rough edges, overall these principles make good practical sense to experienced military professionals. In the field of military ethics in particular, clean and tidy solutions to problems are sometimes at hand, but often all options have some regrettable aspects.[2] Choosing an option, in these circumstances requires learning the profession's vocabulary. It necessitates a deep understanding of the constraints under which the profession carries out its duties. It even requires an understanding of the internal structure and dynamics of the profession. Military ethics have come under greater scrutiny especially during the 'War on Terror and Insurgency'. The question of what constitutes a 'just war' and how it may be waged are highlighted in the conflicts involving security forces in counter-insurgency and anti-terrorist operations.

The Centrality of Ethics to Leadership

Ethics are a fundamental component of leadership. Our lives are permeated with ethical challenges that help each one of us to learn about oneself and the world around us.

Through such experiences we build our character, which is one of the most important elements of leadership. In regard to leadership, ethics has to do with what leaders do and who leaders are. It is concerned with the nature of leaders' behavior, and with their virtuousness. In any decision making situation, ethical issues are either implicitly or explicitly involved. Other leadership elements, like our value systems, the goals that we set for ourselves and for our organizations, our actions, and our interaction and relationships with others, all lead to changes in our environment and contribute to the legacy we leave behind.

Leaders have a particular responsibility to enforce ethical standards because they hold both the power and the responsibility to exert change. Ethical leadership means first and foremost staying true to oneself and remaining firmly grounded in reality, recognizing that we, leaders and subordinates, are all equal in our obligations to respect the same laws and ethical standards. Rank or status immunity does not give us the right to misuse it, and it does not give us absolution from breaking the law. Ethical leadership means to treat others as you would like to be treated yourself: to treat everyone with dignity and respect regardless of their ethnic, religious, or social background, gender or political beliefs, rank or file. It means giving everyone a chance at learning, expression, development, and promotion.

Ethical leadership carries with it an obligation to use power and authority for the common good, to improve the lives of others. It means motivating and leading others to do well and to make a difference for a better world. As human beings, we have a responsibility well beyond our official functions. We have to build professional ethics upon our personal ethics. Fairness, caring, and compassion for others have to lead us in our professional and personal lives. Leaders influence followers and the nature of the influence depends on the leaders' character and behavior (particularly the nature and outcome of behaviors).

Leaders fill positions of command. And much of leadership is about 'taking charge' and 'getting things done'. Besides these practical things, leadership demands character. Other words for character are integrity or conscience. The ideas of conscience and trust illustrate the difference between leadership and command. Leadership is personal; it depends upon people of good character and moral courage, acting in good conscience. Such people inspire trust in those who follow them willingly. Command is positional and with command comes all the power and authority over subordinates that the leader needs to achieve tasks. The nature and scope of command authority varies from appointment to appointment and increases with rank. Leaders have an ethical claim to the authority of command only by unflagging integrity. Leaders bring strength of character to command positions.

Leadership demands an ethical example. Leadership must be ethically disciplined in order to protect the interests and reputation of the Services and its people and ultimately to ensure that they are given a mandate by government to take only certain lives, in certain ways, at certain times and for certain reasons; otherwise service becomes indistinguishable from murder and military professionals will find themselves condemned by the very societies they serve. The end, no matter how worthy, never justifies unethical means. Leaders demonstrate society's ideals and act in accord with the laws and moral codes which separate the unethical application of force from the ethical application of force. All military tasks must be accomplished by ethical means. To quote General Sir John Hackett 'What a bad person cannot be, is a good sailor, soldier or airman' would be very apt. Military institutions thus form a repository of moral resource that should always be a source of strength within the State.[3]

Leader–His Role in Ethical Development Process

Leaders are responsible for the ethical development of followers as well as for the creation of an ethical culture and climate in their unit. Put simply, ethical leaders decide to do what is 'right', reinforce, and role model 'right' for others. They develop followers to have similar capability for ethical thought and action. Ethical/moral development is a life long journey. Thus entry into the Services should only be looked as a way-point and not as a start point or an end state. In fact my own impression is that officers averaging ten years of service are still developing ethically and that on average have yet to achieve the higher levels of ethical development. We must, therefore, take a holistic view and target development throughout a leader's career. Such a development is critical when determining a leader's capability, as followers assess both their character and competence.

If one were to look at the holistic development of a leader, it is traditionally developed in two domains namely, Competence and Character. Competence would include tactical, technical, analytical and inter-personal skills. It results in demonstrated ability to successfully perform one's duties and to accomplish the mission with discipline and to standard. Character on the other hand is a combination of ethics, values and attributes that define a leader as a person. Character is the service professional's dedication and adherence to the services values and the profession's ethic as consistently and faithfully demonstrated in decisions and actions.[4] Thus, a leader's character will influence what his core values are, how he establishes a command climate, how he interprets situations, think about leadership duties and style, what he demands and inspire in followers, the decisions he makes, and most importantly, how he behaves as a leader. This is best explained by the process briefly described as 'Education, Train, Develop and Inspire'. Experience through feedback further consolidates their being leaders of character. The bottom line is that in order to lead effectively especially in extreme situations such as combat, leaders through their decision making skills must earn their subordinates' trust.

The Trilogy of 'Ethics, Conscience and Leadership'

Ethics also means the continuous effort of examining our own moral beliefs and our moral conduct, and striving to ensure that we, and the institutions we help to shape, live up to standards that are reasonable and solidly based. Conscience is an engine of moral authenticity or genuineness, enabling professional decisions from the basis of integrity. Conscience is central to the leadership *ethic of being* which is central to military ethos. Being is what Debashis Chatterjee in his book 'Timeless Leadership' describes being as 'the raw material for becoming a leader'. Character is defined by conscience, which is the moral sense of right and wrong and central to leadership. Leaders acknowledge other people as moral equals, equally deserving of the respect which promotes trust and confidence. This emphasizes those leaders' model professional ideals which demand more than mere technical expertise. Despite all our efforts, the chance of a clash between conscience and duty through ignorance and misjudgment is still very real. The risk is there in peace, it is probably at its height in counter-insurgency, and it smolders in general war. All the while, the soldier's actions are exposed, and his principles questioned by the society as never before. [5]

Conscience, more robust than the 'competencies'

of 'emotional intelligence', is an inner feeling relating to the goodness or otherwise of behavior. Conscience guides behavior and is more than an ill-defined, self-justified confidence in the rightness of action or judgment. Conscience draws upon the wider environment in which it operates. In the Services conscience is strengthened by a rational appreciation of our values, conventions, expectations, and by the ideals of the Services. The rational foundation of conscience is important because leaders must be exemplars of the military profession and inspire others to commit to a just cause. Conscience demands ethical *mindfulness* or ethical *awareness*.[6] Leaders of conscience will always realize what they are doing, and why they are doing it. They will work hard to be ethically responsive and to build an organization which becomes collectively mindful. Ethical leadership does not depend upon the quality and substance of (organizational) values, but upon the strength of character which interprets and applies values to achieve what's best and right. Acting in good conscience is the essence of leadership by example, and fundamental to trust between leaders and followers.

Ethics of Character : Virtues and Values

For Aristotle, virtue is something that is practiced and, thereby, learned – it is a habit. This has clear implications for moral education, for Aristotle obviously thinks that people can be taught to be virtuous. Virtues are those strengths of character that enable us to flourish. A virtuous person has practical wisdom, the ability to know when and how best to apply these various moral perspectives. Values are what we, as a profession, judge to be right. Individually or organizationally, values determine what is right and what is wrong, and doing what is right or wrong is what we mean by ethics. To behave ethically is to behave in a manner consistent with what is right or moral.

Character is the foundation of a leadership culture. Such a culture recognizes that commendable personal example generates trust and commitment, rather than compliance and submission. Such a culture appreciates leadership as the ethical expression of 'power with,' rather than 'power over,' and fosters mutually respectful partnerships, united in the ethical pursuit of missions.

Character, comprised of a person's moral and ethical qualities, helps determine what is right and gives a leader motivation to do what is appropriate, regardless of the circumstances or consequences. An informed ethical conscience consistent with the Services values strengthens leaders to make the right choices when faced with tough issues. Leaders must embody these values and inspire others to do the same.

Character is essential to successful leadership. It determines who people are, how they act, helps determine right from wrong, and choose what is right. Adhering to the principles as embodied in the Services values, is essential to upholding high ethical standards of behavior. Unethical behavior quickly destroys organizational morale and cohesion; it undermines the trust and confidence essential to teamwork and mission accomplishment. Consistently doing the right thing forges strong character in individuals and expands to create a culture of trust throughout the organization.

Ethics indicate how a person should behave. Military values represent the beliefs that a person has. For example the seven Army values of Loyalty, Duty, Respect, Selflessness, Honor, Integrity, and Courage (physical and moral), represent a set of common beliefs that leaders are expected to uphold and reinforce by their actions. The translation from desirable ethics to internal values to actual behavior involves choices. Discipline though not specifically stated above as a core value, is a value which is most profound when it finds expression as self-discipline, a dignified, responsible and willing commitment to the ethos of professional service articulated in our value system.

Ethical conduct must reflect genuine values and beliefs. Services personnel adhere to the military values because they want to live ethically and profess the values because they know what is right. Adopting good values and making ethical choices are essential to produce leaders of character. Leaders seen as abusive or toxic (such as intimidating and insulting subordinates) have higher rates of non-combatant mistreatment and misconduct in their units/establishments. Leaders must consistently focus on shaping ethics-based organizational climates in which subordinates and organizations can achieve their full potential. Leaders, who adhere to applicable laws, regulations, and unit standards, build credibility with their subordinates and enhance trust with the people they serve.

Ethical Dilemmas

A dilemma is a predicament in which the decision-maker must choose between two options of near or equal value. In addition, the dilemmas which confront modern professionals may result from options, which are not well defined, or from solutions, which create additional possible or known problems and harm for the problem carrier or for others. We have all experienced, at one time or another, situations in which our professional responsibilities unexpectedly come into conflict with our deepest values. We very often respond to these in a variety of ways: some impulsively 'go with the gut feeling', others talk it over with friends, colleagues, or families; still others think back to what a mentor would do in similar circumstances. In every case, regardless of what path is chosen, these decisions taken cumulatively over many years form the basis of an individual's character.

Not every ethical dilemma has a right solution. Reasonable people often disagree; otherwise, there would be no dilemma. However, it is essential that one must agree on a process for dealing with dilemmas.[7]

Ethical Reasoning Versus Rationalization

To have clear ethical thought is to discern the difference between *'reasoning'* and *'rationalization'*. Reasoning is a process of analysis for arriving at informed judgments. It clarifies the distinction between right and wrong action. Rationalization is a process of constructing a justification for a decision we suspect is really flawed, and often, one that was arrived at through a mental process characterized by contrivance and self-dealing. Rationalization purposefully blurs right and wrong. We fool ourselves into thinking something is justified when it is not. This is a lesson we all have learned, probably to our embarrassment. But in ethical decision making, rationalization can become more than an isolated error. It can become a habit. With practice, we can ethically desensitize ourselves to the point that we are likely to repeatedly do the wrong thing.[8]

When we rationalize, we devise specious but self-satisfying reasons for acting. Or, ascribe our actions to high-mindedness when our motives are actually otherwise. Or, employ a faulty analogy. In effect, we create a story that holds together, but upon examination, does not hold up. We commonly rationalize to avoid embarrassment, get ahead, or be kind.

The tell tale sayings of rationalizations that pop-up daily are: *"If you can't beat them; join them, if I don't do it, somebody else will; It is all for the good of the organization; If it does not hurt anyone, what does it matter? Everyone else is doing it"*. We can be sure that when we catch such lines on the tips of our tongues, we are twisting ethical reasoning.

Conclusion

The question of ethics is faced in all walks of life. Everywhere it raises hard, often insoluble questions about the choice of the right path. The biggest trouble even to a sincere wish to conform to ethical principles is the persistent cropping of situations where ethical principles themselves may appear to be contradictory and one has to make a difficult choice, guided by one's conscience. Conscience is probably best described as a fallible moral judgment which, if acknowledged, produces actions and if ignored, merely produces a sense of guilt. An informed ethical conscience consistent with our value systems strengthens leaders to make right choices when faced with tough issues.

A leader is a moral 'exemplar', in that he demonstrates ethical behavior in all his actions both in public and private. He embeds these ethical behaviors in all his decisions and knows and recognizes how these actions affect the common good. Not only is he aware of the core values, he also has the courage to live these throughout of his life. Here he moves from the 'mere intellectual acceptance' to a 'heart and soul embodiment' of these values in every day decisions and actions, thus, articulating 'walking the talk'. He will not compromise the good of the whole for the privilege of the select few. What makes the leader the most is certain solidity at the core, based on principles that are essential points on a moral compass.

Making good ethical decisions requires a trained sensitivity to ethical issues and a practiced method for exploring the ethical aspects of a decision and weighing the considerations that impact the choice of a course of action. Making ethical decisions is easy when the facts are clear and the choices black and white. But it is a different story when the situation is clouded by ambiguity, incomplete information, multiple points of view, and conflicting responsibilities.

Many cases of misconduct, cheating, misappropriation, bribery, though may appear different, have a lot in common since they are full of the oldest questions in the world-questions of human behavior and human judgment applied in ordinary day–to-day situations. Clay T. Buckingham puts it more succinctly when he remarks 'Standing firm ethically can exact a cost, perhaps a steep one. As professionals we must be willing to pay it.'[9] It is good to remember that as a leader if we fail to properly inform, train, or prepare our soldiers, we will neither be positioned for success nor empowered with the requisite insight to make discerning judgments. Similarly, if we fail to inculcate, demonstrate, and police the values and beliefs inherent in the Service ethos, our personnel will be denied the ethical certainty they require to know what 'right looks like' and to do their 'duty with discernment.'[10]

References

1. Martin L. Cook & Henrik Syse (2010): What Should We Mean by 'Military Ethics'? *Journal of Military Ethics*, 9:2, pp 119-122.
2. Bill Rhodes-"*An Introduction to Military Ethics-A Reference Handbook*"-Chapter 1-'An Overview of Applied Ethics for the Military',pp2-3
3. Sir John Hacket in "The Military in the Service of the State in Malham M. Wakin- "*War, Morality and Military Profession*", pp 124-5.
4. 'Facilitating Professional character development using Stories, Vignettes and Case Studies, Chapter II-Professional Character Development' , at Center for the Army Profession and Ethic, 30 Sep 2013.
5. James Glover in "A Soldier and his Conscience" in "*Parameters of Military Ethics*", PERGAMON-BRASSEY'S International Defence Publishers.Inc, pg 149.

6. The Royal Australian Navy-Leadership Ethics-2010, Chapter 1-'Leaders of Conscience', pp 17-24.
7. Joseph L. Badaracco, Jr in "The Discipline of Building Character"- *Harvard Business Review* on Leadership, pp 80-113.
8. Ronald A. Howard and Clinton D. Korver in "*Ethics for the Real World*"--Chapter 2 –'Draw Distinctions' pp 43-44.
9. Clay.T. Buckingham, "Ethics and the Senior Officer: Institutional Tensions", Autumn Issue 1985 of *Parameters*.
10. Lt.Gen Andrew Leslie, CMM,MSC,MSM,CD, Chief of Land Staff/Army Commander-'Duty with discernment(Good judgment with insight)-CLS guidance on ethics in operation-Canada National Defence.

5

Essence of Ethical Leadership at Senior Ranks

"Talk to people in their own language. If you do it well, they'll say, 'God, he said exactly what I was thinking.' And when they begin to respect you, they'll follow you always."

Lee Iacocca

Introduction

The above quote highlights the fact that leaders make a difference in the way they communicate with those who follow them. Leaders inspire followers to act and sacrifice. Leaders motivate people and organizations to make changes and tackle challenges. Leaders come in countless varieties, and differ from one another in style, personality, and methods. Nevertheless, there is a common distinguishing characteristic among all leaders who are truly effective: they have tremendous influence upon the lives and work of others. Leaders are shapers of values, creators, interpreters of institutional purpose, exemplars, makers of meanings, path finders, and molders of organizational culture. They are persistent and consistent.[1] Such things obviously come from a deep sense of purpose and a sense of overall direction. The very act of assuming responsibility for guiding, directing, or controlling others pre-supposes a moral responsibility for goals, missions, and methods. A leader does not exist for his individual personal value, but for his ability to show the way and make his men want to follow. This is indeed the core of the leader's existence, and without it no hope exists of grappling with the tasks of command. It is seen at its simplest in warlike operations, but the power to lead smoothes the way of every task in every branch of a military organization, whether in war or peace. It breathes vitality into an organization that will take a collection of men, materials, and machines, and waken them to purposeful, effective life.

Unlike other professions, the profession of arms is practiced in the chaotic and deadly machinations of war. To be effective in combat, the Services need its members to have a self-perception of warriors as fighters; and the army as a whole needs to be imbued with the characteristic spirit, an ethos of the fighting warrior, the drive to close with the enemy and kill him. A strong warrior ethos is, thus, a precious commodity.[2] Closer the leader is to the battle, with the consequent, greater risk to life, the more dynamic and decisive the leader will need to be.

Authentic, transformational, and ethical leadership is at the heart of our military profession. Leaders at all levels set the ethical tone for subordinates in their units either by omission or commission and have a significant impact on how their subordinates act and perform. Indeed, leaders are often the most important source of inspiration that subordinates look up to for guidance in their behaviors. Engaging in ethical leadership is among the most important components of leadership. A senior officer/leader or officer in senior ranks as it appears in this chapter implies, 'he is at the pinnacle of hierarchy, and wields considerable influence over his subordinates and the professional environment.'[3]

Salient Attributes of Ethical Leadership

"You must know that it is no easy thing for a principle to become a man's own, unless each day he maintains it and hear it maintained, as well as work it out in life."

Epictetus (A Greek Philosopher, circa 50-130 AD)

Researchers in the field of applied psychology define ethical leadership as the 'demonstration of appropriate conduct through personal actions and relationships and the promotion of such conduct to subordinates through two-way communication, reinforcement, and decision making.'[4]

This definition highlights three key components of ethical leadership. First, leaders become credible and authentic ethical role models by engaging in behaviors that subordinates deem unselfish and ethically appropriate. These behaviors include being honest, showing consideration for others, and treating people fairly and with respect. Ethical leadership entails engaging in transparent, fair, and caring actions. By doing so, leaders become an example of how to behave and a model for others to identify with and imitate. This is an ongoing process; subordinates are continuously evaluating their leaders, so a leader who is ethical at one point in time and not at another sends mixed messages that damage his authenticity.

Second, ethical leadership entails directing attention

to ethical issues and standards. Services personnel, like all people, have only a finite attention span and a lot of competing information to process. Ethical leadership requires emphasizing the importance and significance of ethics. Communicating about ethics on a consistent basis is a key component to ethical leadership; leaders who behave ethically but never talk to their subordinates about ethics will fall short in ethical leadership.

Third, ethical leadership entails creating ethical command climates that set the conditions for positive outcomes and ethically appropriate behavior and provide negative outcomes for inappropriate behavior. Subordinates pay close attention to rewards and punishment, and they quickly learn to engage in behavior that gains rewards and avoids punishment. It is also important that they perceive the rewards and punishment process as fair, or the leader loses credibility.[5]

Ethical leadership is a two-way process.[6] Ethical leaders must direct attention to ethical issues, enforce ethical standards, and allow subordinates to bring up ethical issues with them. Rewards and punishments should take place in an environment of open two-way communication. Subordinates must inform their leaders about ethical issues they may face (that the leader is unaware of), and ethical leaders must clearly inform the followers about ethical standards.

Moral Challenges to a Commander

"Man has a natural aptitude for virtue; but perfection of virtue must be acquired by man by means of some kind of training."

Saint Thomas Aquinas.

Some of the key tests of a senior leader are in his capacity and diligence to face the hazards and problems of: [7]

Living with Compromise

Senior leaders in any organization even of modest complexity must live on a diet of compromise. Leadership rests on an amalgamation of opinion, a fusion of standards. A healthy organization encourages differences and originality of judgment. All this is good but it makes for everyday aches and pains. There will be conflicts of interest. For one thing, one must choose between long term and short term values. Sometimes a conflict between individual and institutional values would need to be resolved. Also some compromises are those that balance material and non-material values. There are some benefits in compromise. Often, it is the only way to secure group action. The price of diverse opinion/ wisdom among differing people may be mutual adjustment before action is possible. Further, such compromise educates differing individuals. In the end, compromise may be the way ideals actualize themselves. Perhaps, the chief evil in compromise lies in its apparent disregard of universal principle. A leader undermines his own influence if he becomes motivated largely by expediency. Virtue remains largely a habit of the will to follow principle. Deviation from principle may become habit forming. Fear of mediocrity, short sightedness, and unpredictability sets in when principle falls out.

Control of Truth

Another moral hazard besetting the senior leader resides in his control of truth on many occasions. It is rare that he has the privilege of telling the truth, the whole truth and nothing but the truth. To take a common illustration, truth bluntly told may hurt a subordinate who is incompetent or misguided. When improvement by this subordinate is possible, tactful treatment of the fault to be corrected would involve some adroit selection of truths that can be told.

So far so good. But if he withholds truth on this occasion, he might do so on other occasions. Can he be trusted to withhold the *right* truths?

And let us not delude ourselves about the frequency with which these occasions occur in and out of the office. No leader can escape all of them. The leader has to look to the orientation of the truth he chooses to emphasize. Here integrity becomes an essential requirement of the leader. He can be trusted with the direction of his organization only if he is able to interrelate in one whole, all of its affairs. He must see the whole truth about the operations of his institution, and handle the partial truths called on each occasion by reference to this whole. A person of integrity is a fully integrated person. He can become so and remain so, only by constant regard for the whole system of facts he knows—those he does not disclose as well as those he does.

Finality of Decisions

The third moral dilemma for the senior leader arises from the many occasions when his judgment alone must be taken as final. Broad matters of policy are usually set by people high-up in hierarchy, but these are often recommended by the subordinate commanders, and when approved, they are interpreted and applied by him. Often responsibility for a decision can be lodged nowhere else. Some subordinates relish freedom from basic decisions and delight in passing them up the line of command. The senior most leader/ commander is indeed 'the recipient of the final buck'. Lack of time/immediacy often requires decisions before all the facts are in or can be obtained. It would be nothing but an act of genius to reach the conclusions before all the facts are in. A leader is often called on to be such a genius. He dare not be wrong, though it may be his own judgment alone he can trust. If he is wrong, the disaster may be overwhelming.

A responsible leader seeks counsel where possible.

But some problems cannot be discussed with others. For instance, financial and personal questions are sometimes so confidential as to require complete secrecy. One must avoid bias, both seeming and real. A measure of aloofness becomes the price of objectivity. Certain unavoidable loneliness is attached, consequently,to administrative leadership. If this loneliness becomes apparent to colleagues, the boss finds himself an object of pity and a cause of hushed conversations on his approach. One must like his job however severe the discipline of issues one must handle alone. Presumably the leader is one of the best informed people in his organization and to stay so one must demand of every subordinate information, in relevant form about one's task or mission. But the leader's chief need is for help on problems no one else knows much about. He will find searching for principles to guide him where his judgment alone is required. And the fulcrum of one's judgment comes at last to be a scheme of values.

Responsibility for Errors

Some hazards come in the form of responsibility for the mistakes of a subordinate. Originality and initiative are essential in the subordinates of a healthy organization. Experimentation brings fresh inputs and values. Delegated authority implies that a subordinate has the right to make mistakes and the duty to accept responsibility for his mistakes. Responsibility given to subordinates obviously matures their judgment. They learn from their mistakes. The moral issue emerges when these failures mount to such proportions that they become expensive or harmful to the prestige of the institution or to the welfare of the colleagues. Certainly there are limits for going on assuming responsibility for the serious errors of subordinates.No senior leader can administer on an atomistic theory of morals. It is both right and expedient, therefore, that the senior leader assumes some responsibility for the errors of his subordinates. If they cannot be corrected, senior's obligation cease and a new person must be put on the job. Sound administration depends for its success on common aims individually shared. The confidant leader stands in a position of mutual influence with his subordinates. He may judge and discipline them when they err, if he has developed for himself sufficiently reliable standards of private judgment.

However, his judgment will consist largely in continuously setting before them high standards of excellence with which they cannot fail to compare themselves. Their inability or ability to reach these standards will generally become so apparent to themselves and their colleagues that they will respond with better effort.

Images and Mirages

The Commander' or possibly the person aspiring to succeed to that position, is called upon to live up to, or fit into, an image of the head of the organization that is pre-established in most cases. Such personnel must present success and confidence in the future. 'The good of the establishment' often comes ahead of personal pleasures or convenience. Another problem, strange as may seem, is that the office of the leader often receives a great deal of recognition and praise. The danger is that the leader may be deceived into receiving this recognition for himself rather than his office. As awards, citations, and publicity come to him for his organization, as if he had done the work himself, it is a subtle temptation to forget that he is the mouthpiece only of his establishment, and not the whole body. If he accepts recognition and achievements of his office as his own, he may remove himself from the discriminating critics and ride unjustly on the shoulders of his colleagues' achievement. He must, therefore, come back once more to his own scheme of professional and moral values.

Ethical Fault Lines at Senior Ranks

"At the center of your being you have the answer; you know who you are and you know what you want."

Lao Tzu in 'Tao Te Ching (The book of the Way)

The nature of the military system in itself is able to breed some of the ethical dilution. This is an area of special concern; especially, the tensions that confront senior officers turn out to be fertile grounds for ethical abuse. All military officers have experienced these tensions and they will continue to characterize the environment in which senior officers serve. As one progress, the higher the position or rank, the more complex and less precise are the issues, less subject to specific rules and simple solutions. To withstand these tensions, a senior leader needs to be bedrock of ethical values. Some very specific issues which he would have to address for are: [8]

- **Use of Authority**—We are all aware of the authoritative structure of our profession, even though essential, is the natural breeding ground for unethical use of authority. The higher we go, the easier it is to misuse our authority. The checks and balances we were subjected as junior officers become less evident and less compelling. We gradually begin to feel that we do not need to seek the counsel of others. We are first surprised by and then pleased by the freedom of actions accorded to us. Associated with each rank, of course, are the various levels of responsibility. The question we need to reflect on is 'Am I using my authority, my rank, fully, but solely for the purpose of carrying out my responsibilities?' As we go up in rank, those of lower grade tend more readily to assume that authority is being used legitimately and ethically, because of the high regard with which juniors hold their senior ranks. This brings us to the guts of the use of authority. One of the widespread and patently unethical uses of authority is the exploitation and degradation of subordinates. The higher we go, the more important it is to be careful that our impact on the lives, careers, and families of our subordinates is positive, and healthy and not negative.

- **Rationalization of our Indiscretions**—We tend to rationalize small personal indiscretions that we would never accept in a subordinate. Sometimes we begin to believe that we are somehow above the law and they didn't have a person of our status and responsibility in mind when they wrote it. We then divert funds, misappropriate them etc. It has been generally observed that 'General' officers do not get relieved for incompetence. They get fired for indiscretions, which is simply another way of saying that they have used their authority unethically. As the saying goes 'The higher you go on the Flag pole, the more your rear end shows'. [9]
- **Financial Mis-management**—This has been of late an area of great concern especially with the amount of money now available for operational purposes. The military leader charged with fund/ money management responsibilities may not feel the current rules/procedures are realistically compatible with the business world of today. Occasionally, he may be tempted to renounce or modify the code for himself for the moment. The area of money management has always been fraught with great pressures and temptation. Where large sums of money are involved or business interests are brought to bear, there is a possibility of conflict

between ethical codes of the business world and those of military profession. Quite often one may get involved in procurement functions, authorizing local purchase, purchases of 'Commercially off the Shelf' (COTS) equipments, etc. All too often, the unsuspecting officer finds himself in the position of being trapped into receiving favors from persons with whom he is doing business before he realized that they fully expect something in return. What to them is a legitimate business expense in promoting sales of their product can be a concealed form of bribery to the officer. This weakens his moral position of impartiality and objectivity in office. For this reason, the code reinforced by regulations and rules protects the officer by requiring him not to place himself in a position of not accepting personal favors when he is doing business or allowing his personal interests to be involved or appear to be involved in these transactions. Frequently, the mere appearance of personal involvement can be as damaging to his position as actual involvement.

- **Difference between Honesty and Deception**— This is another tension which confronts all of us as we progress in life. One of the most common deceptions is the exaggeration of the need to get what is really needed, knowing that the initial request is certainly going to be reduced. Money is usually the object. In fact, this sort of thing happens even at the highest level. The higher the careerists rise, the more they see their role as protectors of service traditions, doctrine, and loyalties. Service parochialism continues to dominate the defense planning and programming process though one is hopeful that the 'battle of the turf' has somewhat reduced with the setting up of Headquarters, Integrated Defence Staff (IDS). With sincere efforts towards jointmanship, the mystique of budget shares and force structure maintenance would be looked into and the distrust, if any, would be eliminated. While a joint perspective is not absent from the considerations of requirements for future forces, it remains subordinate to that of individual services at a time when each recognizes increasing budget constraints and believes it is involved in a zero-sum funding contest. Today we face duplication generated not only by service redundancy, but by increasing number of defense agencies which have become additional competitors for resources. Here one would comment on the Annual Confidential Report (ACR) system, where ethical principles of honesty surface while rating one's subordinates honestly when others are inflating reports of their subordinates. Is it fair to wage a one man campaign for strict honesty when it is at the expense of my people? i.e. the dilemma of honestly appraising an officer with whom one has and will maintain intimate professional and social contact. Dilemmas between tact and truthfulness, loyalty and sycophancy also confront many.

- **Inability to Handle Success**—Many ethical violations by successful senior officers are by-products of success and not necessarily only due to competitive pressures. Being poorly prepared to deal with success may tend them to become complacent and lose focus, thus, diverting attention to things other than leading. Success whether personal or organizational often leads to privileged access to information, people, or objects. With success usually comes increasingly unrestrained control of organizational resources. And, finally success can inflate such a person's belief in his personal ability to manipulate outcomes.

The Way Forward- Enhancing The Ethical Climate

"It's not enough to espouse high standards. To live up to them – and help others to do the same – requires an ethical cast of mind that lets you practice your principles consistently."

'The Ethical Mind' – Howard Gardner

As a senior officer/leader, your responsibility for upholding the highest standards of ethical conduct does not merely end with your compliance. Seniors have also have leadership functions that include creating a culture of high ethical standards, performance with integrity, maintaining and enhancing a work environment that encourages subordinates to raise concerns without fear of retaliation and promptly addressing ethical violations or misconduct. We also need to examine ways to enhance the prevalent ethical climate in each one's sphere of influence for greater involvement in our organizational approaches so that everyone can feel both a sense of personal values and responsibility for the part they play. To meet this challenge, few best practices are being suggested in the succeeding paragraphs.

Leading by example: Modeling the way

This is something akin to what we refer to in the Services namely 'Leading from the Front'. Many examples of this come to our mind especially our young officers and their saga of courage and valor in the Kargil conflict. The iconic slogan of '*DIL MANGE MORE*' of Late Captain Vikram Batra, PVC (posthumous) still rings loud and clear in our ears. Titles and appointments are granted-we not only know but also recognize them. But it is our behavior that wins us respect. Leading means that we have to be a good example and live what we say. Exemplary leaders know that if they want to gain commitment and achieve the highest standards, they must be models of the behavior they expect of others. To effectively model the behavior they expect of others, senior leaders must first be clear about guiding principles. They must clarify values. Leaders need to open up their hearts and let people know what they really think and believe. This means talking about their values. As a leader especially at the senior ranks, we must find our own voice and then we must clearly and distinctly give voice to these values which we aspire. But it is not just the leaders' values that are important. They are not just representing themselves. They speak and act on behalf of a larger organization. Leaders must forge agreement around common principles and ideals. Some, if not many, military leaders do not lead effectively. They hold a title and they are figureheads at the head of the pack. Their leadership is a facade and there is little of substance behind the mask of authority defined by the badge of rank. Clothes of authority, however, cannot in themselves generate either ability or effectiveness as a leader. Clearly, the abilities and effectiveness of any leader are only as strong as are perceived by those who are led.

Eloquent speeches about common values, however, are not nearly enough. Leaders' deeds are for more important than their words when one wants to determine how serious leaders are about what they say. Words and deeds must be consistent. Exemplary leaders go first. They go first by setting the *example* through daily actions that demonstrate that they are deeply committed to their beliefs. Modeling the way is about earning the right and respect to lead through direct involvement and action. People follow first the person, then the plan.

Strengthening your credibility

Leaders don't get extraordinary things done all by themselves! The portrayal can be completed only when we add in that, what our followers expect from their leaders. With these brush strokes, the picture takes on depth and vitality. A survey questionnaire called "Characteristics of Admired Leaders" was administered to thousands of business and government executives, who were confronted with the question, 'what values, personal traits, or characteristics do you look for and admire in a leader?' From the responses duly analyzed, consistently across countries, cultures, ethnicities, organizational functions and hierarchies, gender, educational, and age groups, it emerged that for people to follow someone willingly (the key word in this question being 'willingly', not because they have to, but because they want to), the majority of the respondents believe that leaders must be *Honest, Forward looking, Inspiring and Competent.*[10] These attributes reinforce and act as complementary perspectives. Putting it all together, it only reinforces the fact that credibility is the foundation of leadership. As it is often remarked, 'if you don't believe in the messenger, you won't believe the message'. Many things contribute to credibility: the track record of the person delivering the message, the content of the message itself, the communicator's reputation for integrity and trustworthiness, and the consistency between words and deeds.

Credibility goes far beyond follower attitudes. It makes a difference, and leaders must take it personally. Loyalty, commitment, energy, and excellence depend on it. The question that often arises in our minds is 'What is credibility behaviorally? How do you know it when you see it?' Some of the phrases people use to describe how they know credibility when they see it are:

- "They practice what they preach."
- "They Walk the Talk".
- "Their actions are consistent with their words."

- "They follow through on their promises".
- "They do what they say they will do".

An acronym –*DWYSYWD*, which stands for *Do what you say you will do,* would best sum up what has been stated above.[11] This practice includes the clarification of a set of values and being an example of those values to others. The consistent living out of values is a behavioral way of demonstrating honesty and trust worthiness. People trust leaders when their deeds and words match.[12] Having values is very important, but it is much more important to live them. 'Walking the talk' is always one of our greatest challenges.

Creating Ethical Environments

This aspect assumes great significance in these times. Our leaders need to be ethical as well as predictable. Media reports of stage- managed encounters, killing of terrorists, senior leaders looking towards civil courts for resolving promotion-related issues, and human rights violations are but some indications of the broader decline of values and principles. There has been a general decline of values all over and it is seriously affecting the moral fibre of our leaders. Ethics is a critical component of any organization's climate. The Services make it plain that it expects leaders at all levels to be ethical standard-bearers. Every leader is charged with building an ethical climate in his or her unit that demands and rewards behavior consistent with Services values.

The ethical climate is the pervasive characteristic of our Services that affects how decisions are made. The health of ethical climate is based on a soldier's perception of how leadership does business and constitutes a shared perception of 'right behavior.' If we permit a vacuum between what we profess and what we practice, the soldier will identify and fill the incongruence between the normative (the way things are right now) and the way things should be. Leaders must exhibit the decision making skills, knowledge, and competencies to make ethically sound decisions. Credibility of leadership at all levels is essential in ensuring an ethical climate. While command responsibility is legal 'authority in war,' subordinates will only follow ethical leadership by personal example. If ambiguity and uncertainty are the hallmarks of asymmetrical warfare, then the task is to instill ethical clarity through the inculcation, demonstration, and policing of the Services values.

Affirming Shared Values

Shared values do make a significant positive difference in work attitudes and performance. They encourage ethical behavior and foster teamwork and esprit-de- corps. They promote higher levels of loyalty and foster pride in the unit/ establishment/formation. Once people are clear about the leader's values, about their own values, and about shared values, they know what is expected of them, can manage higher levels of stress, and can better handle the conflicting demands of work and their personal lives. Senior leaders have more control over the professional environment than they may realize. If we communicate our commitment of our high standards to our fellow officers, they will be more likely to respect those standards in their dealings with us. If we form alliances with like-minded peers, the solidarity of our joint commitment to high standards can improve the organization's professionalism. If we detect unethical practices and devise other more acceptable ways to get the mission accomplished, we can change undesirable patterns of behavior. If we are generous in recognizing highly professional performance, even (or especially) on the part of those with whom we are in professional competition, we can build new bonds of shared commitment to high standards. And, if when it may become necessary, we stand up to be counted in refusing to compromise our standards, we set an example that seniors, peers, and subordinates alike can take counsel from.

Enforcing Ethical Standards and its Compliance

Senior leaders must not only exemplify service values in their words and deeds, they must create the opportunity for everyone under their command to live them as well. It is important for the seniors at all levels to foster an ethical climate by making ethical expectations clear, discussing ethical concerns, dealing with ethical risks, and ensuring a reprisal free environment in their own area/zone of influence. Leaders must respond quickly and aggressively to signs of illegal or unethical behavior. Ethical violations are not just mistakes; they are fundamental failings in our profession of arms. Leaders/seniors must be committed to perform their assigned duties with discipline and to standards, and to strive to successfully and ethically accomplish the mission despite adversity, obstacles, and challenge. Enforcing ethical standards is the legitimate responsibility of senior leaders. They should encourage subordinates to speak about ethics and compliance issues and concerns, thereby, highlighting that ethics and compliance are an integral part of decision making.

Coaching, Mentoring and Counseling

The emphasis on coaching is to facilitate the subordinates' individual skills development and consequently improved personal performance. After all until everybody is the best they can be, the organization cannot be the best it needs to be. Mentoring grows from an informal review and reflection process and the sharing of the mentor's personal experience. The Services values of loyalty, duty and selfless service require the leaders to counsel their subordinates. The values of honor, integrity, and personal courage require giving team members straightforward feedback. Of particular concern is the tendency to defend the 'good soldier' euphemism whereby we may tolerate particular soldiers, supported by others, for being 'good in the field', but who are, in fact, simply soldiers of bad character pursuing an alternate ethos based on the values of cruelty, abuse of power, and disrespect for the law. These may be the miscreants who fill a leadership vacuum and lead others astray. The aim of mentoring and counseling is not only to turn such misguided people to be good, but also to provide the leadership, group structure, and the requisite supervision to deny the opportunity for those soldiers of dubious personal character to violate the Services ethos. Regular, effective counseling is an essential part of ethical development, and responsibility for this lies largely on the shoulders of senior ranks who would be expected to passing the baton of their life experiences to those that are learning.

Voicing the Truth

Leadership without truth is like a tree with no roots. It will stand for a while, but as the winds of challenge and change begin to blow, it will fall as people learn it has no living legitimacy. It also means to do as you say you would do, to be consistent with your words and actions. Another cliché that means the same thing is: 'practice what you preach'. It is the opposite of being a hypocrite. There are countless examples in government; the private and public sector organizations to suggest that 'voicing the truth' is not always lived out, surely contributing to the current crisis of leadership. Exemplary leaders are very mindful of the signals they send and how they send them. [13]

Interestingly, in the generally talked about arena of 'authentic' conversation with followers and subordinates, more and more people are not prepared to settle for less and as an institution, we cannot afford anything but the truth. A genuine dialogue implies involving people coming together not to merely 'discuss' their opinion on an issue but rather to share their values and basic assumptions in order to seek deeper meaning and understanding of themselves and their colleagues. In doing so, they connect at a more profound level developing an 'espirit-de-corps' which is very important for us in the Services. Leaders voicing the truth are able to inspire many numbers and are surprised sometimes as to 'where the words come from'. Whatever the experience, it is often profound and always refreshing when the 'truth' is present in our lives.

Trusting Inner Knowing-Seeking Spiritual Support

As the outside world becomes interestingly unstable, people are beginning to turn inward to find answers to life's deeper questions. In making the commitment to this inner exploration, people are discovering that they have access to a wealth of wisdom they are learning to trust. In recent years more credence has been given to this inward journey in our lives. So what exactly is the inner journey and how does it present itself? There are many ways to describe it and just as many ways of experiencing it.[14] Our choices of ethical, and the exceptions to standards stem from the particularities of our inner voice, not someone else's. The '*conscience*', the '*quite voice*' from *within*' or '*intuition*' is an inner form of teaching. Acting in good conscience is the essence of leadership by example, and fundamental to trust between leaders and followers.

Imagine ourselves in front of a mirror which does not blind us to the failings of our personality. This objective mirror, we should use it mentally to see the least machinery of our character, its weaknesses and its secretiveness. We will no longer be able for convenience's sake, disregard unsatisfactory aspects of our personality. When this thorough soul searching bears its fruit, we will feel as if we have been given a new lease of life, that we will make our life both internally and externally richer, and be an effective leader. It helps us to think deeply enough to identify nuanced ethical issues for ourselves. [15]

It is in seeking an understanding of their evolving spirituality that soldiers and leaders will form and re-enforce their self-identity, find their sense of purpose and meaning in life, form their own philosophy for viewing the world and develop standards that define how to live a good life. Regardless of the approach to addressing spirituality, whether it is through religion, the study of philosophy or ethics, the arts, nature, or other means, leaders at all levels must establish clear core beliefs and values and uphold their beliefs with conviction to be ethical and moral leaders'--leaders' of character.

Handling of Success

Some advice to successful leaders is warranted:

- **Firstly,** it could happen to you. Stand forewarned and read the papers for constant reminders that the chances of being caught have never been greater.
- **Secondly,** realize that living a balanced life reduces the likelihood of the negatives of success causing you to lose touch with reality. Family, relationships, and interests other work must be cultivated for a long-term success to be meaningful.
- **Thirdly,** understand that your primary function is to provide strategic direction and leadership at all levels. Avoid becoming complacent with strategic direction and current performance. Strategic direction is never 'set', no matter how successful. The privilege and status that has been granted is designed to enhance your strategic vision. It is not a reward for a job already accomplished. Likewise, control of organizational resources has been given to you so that you can execute strategy—not feed personal gratification.
- **Fourthly,** build an ethical team of people around

you who will inspire you to lead by example and who will challenge or comfort you when you need either.

- **Finally,** ethical leadership is simply a part of good leadership and requires focus, the appropriate use of resources, trust, effective decision making and provision of model behaviour that is worth following. Once it is lost it is difficult, if not impossible, to regain. If success leads to increased levels of power, then we must take steps to deal with the phenomenon that 'power corrupts'. We must always look out for creative ways to prevent this from occurring while not limiting the ability of leaders to lead.

Conclusion

In a major embarrassment for the Services, some senior top ranking officers have recently come under the scanner in a number of cases ranging from embezzlement to sexual harassment. Some feel that cases of corruption at higher levels in the Services are perhaps an indicator of a deeper systemic malaise. This needs tackling the root cause of the malady, and not stopping at only treating the symptoms. The long-term solution is to undertake systemic reform. This will require follow up besides at the Services level but also call for lot of political will. As most of the cases are sub-judice, we must not be tempted to pass quick judgments.

Mahatma Gandhi is reported to have said that there is enough on this earth to meet the needs of all, but not the greed of all. If greed, as has been argued by some, is the root of the crisis, then tackling it is a task beyond finance and even economics. This has also do with the ethical moorings of concerned persons. The transition from 'need' to 'greed' along with the acquisitive nature of humans may well be one of the reasons for such indiscretions.

Finally, this chapter has been written not to give any final answers to many of the ethical dilemmas especially any senior officer or a leader faces, but as an agenda worthy of consideration and reflection. No one would have all the answers, but it is hoped that this essay would provide a common base for all to act ethically. In these extraordinary times, there is no shortage of challenges; they seem to only increase in number and complexity. The abundance of challenges is not the issue. It is how we respond to them that matters. One would have also realized that leadership development is indeed 'self-development'. Meeting the leadership challenge is a personal and a daily challenge for all of us. We know that if you have the will and the way to lead, you can. You have to supply the will.

As we move along the path of career advancement, frequent azimuth checks with our ethical compass would be very beneficial and important. By assiduous practice and edifying our ethical behavior, we would encourage others who are seeking the same process. Set a personal example of our ethical conduct as we would serve a great cause in the process of transformation. Our steadfastedness will build a strong edifice of ethical leadership. There must be a demonstrated trust that stated beliefs equate to actual practices. As seniors we influence, we have an effect on others, which means, we need to pay attention to our values and our ethics.

References

1. Egan, G (1985), *Change agent skills.* Monterey, CA:Brooks/Cole
2. "Post-Modern Challenges for Modern Warriors" by John Kiszely—The SHRIVENHAM Papers, No 5, Dec 2007.
3. "Development of an Officer during various stages of Service"-Section 3. pg 11, "Code of Conduct for

Officers", Army Training Note ATN/I/LMS/99 issued by HQ ARTRAC, 12 Jun 99.

4. "What does Contemporary Science say about Ethical Leadership?' by Christopher M. Barnes, Ph D and Lt Col Joseph Doty, Ph D—*Military Review*-Army Ethic 2010.
5. *Ibid.*
6. *Ibid.*
7. "Moral Hazards of an Executive" by Louis William Norris- *Harvard Business Review*–'Ethics for Executives'-Number 1.041.
8. "Code of Conduct for Officers", Army Training Note ATN/I/LMS/99 issued by HQ ARTRAC, 12 Jun 99.
9. "Ethics and the Senior Officer" by Clay T. Buckingham, pp 87-102 in '*Parameters of Military ethics*' , edited by Lloyd J. Matthews and Dale E. Brown—Pergamon Brasseys, International Defence Publications, Inc
10. "Credibility is the Foundation of Leadership" in '*Leadership Challenge*', pp 27-41, by James M.Kouzes & Barry Z. Posner.4th Edition,
11. *ibid*, pp 40-41.
12. "*Personify the Shared Values*" in 'Leadership Challenge', pg 79, by James M.Kouzes & Barry Z. Posner.4th Edition.
13. "*Student Leadership Challenge: Five Practices for Exemplary Leaders*", pg 39, by James M.Kouzes & Barry Z. Posner,John Wiley & Sons,2009.
14. "Sustaining Motivation for Self- Development to be a Leader" pp121-125, in '*Sai Baba's Mahavakya on Leadership*' by Padma Bhushan Lt Gen Dr ML Chibber, PVSM, AVSM , Ph D, (retd.) 1994.
15. "Army Values and Ethics: A Search for consistency and Relevance" by John W. Brinsfield, from '*Parameters*', Autumn, pp 69-84.

PART-II

Ethics in Practice

6

Ethical Issues in Asymmetrical Warfare*

"Asymmetrical warfare presents on a spatial, functional, temporal, and moral plane. Within an information warfare construct, the moral component of asymmetrical warfare has proven to be an operational imperative. Achieving the ethical certainty of acceptable norms of conduct is an all-ranks function. It is analogous to a tug-of-war team whereby ethics and leadership are two strands of the same rope. A failure in either leads to both failing the mission and failing our soldiers".

(Excerpts from 'Duty with Discernment', CLS guidance on Ethics in Operations- Strategic Edition)

(*Published in 'The War College Journal', Volume 43, Summer 2014, pp7-13)

Introduction

The term 'Asymmetric Warfare' is frequently used to describe what is also called 'Guerilla Warfare', 'Insurgency',

'Terrorism', 'Counter-Terrorism', 'Counter-Insurgency', essentially violent conflict between a formal military power and an informal, less equipped and supported, undermanned but a resilient opponent.[1] Weak opponents will use almost any means at their disposal to achieve their aims in war; they will employ terrorist tactics, attack civilians, plant road side bombs , and kill prisoners if they happen to capture any. Such opponents, although not abiding by the Laws of Warfare, will challenge any perceived transgressions on the part of the state actor and exploit it in the court of international public opinion. They will even provoke such transgressions by using human shields around high value targets. Many have tried to describe this new type of warfare and many catch phrases and buzzwords have come and gone more so because it is multi-dimensional and amorphous. It is best described as 'population -centric and non-traditional'.

Asymmetry has many ingredients to include: Material, Technological, Doctrinal, Psychological, Organizational, Training and leadership, Will and Patience.[2] The term 'Asymmetrical Warfare' over the years has undertaken new and broader dimensions but in this paper, it is confined to its usage to describe a number of terrorist related threats and activities. It also pertains to 'Counter-insurgency warfare', wherein, terror is employed by an irregular adversary as a means to subvert the rule of law and effect change through violence and fear. This trend has blurred the distinction between an insurgent and a terrorist. Hence, in this essay, the noun 'terrorist' will be used to describe all armed cadres of an insurrectionist movement. Ethical issues addressed in the paper are based on the author's observations while serving in the North East (NE) and Jammu and Kashmir (J&K).

Defining "Ethics Battlespace"

Battlespace is a term well understood by Services personnel. One of its derivatives in the ethical domain could be termed as 'Ethical battlespace.' It highlights the personal, professional, culture/climate, operational and/or legal influences of professionals' thoughts and behavior within an ethical situation. Some of these influences are internal to the person: human spirit, personal ethics, etc. Some are external: culture/climate, laws, Service norms, etc. These factors compete for an individual's attention when they are placed in situations that have moral and/or ethical implications.[3] Different soldiers may weigh the influence of each of these factors separately. Some soldiers may tend to be guided more by rules of engagement and laws, while others may draw from internal sources of their spirit, while yet others seek to comply with the norms and expectations of their unit members. Regardless of such weightings, it is clear that a framework for ethical development for ethical decision making must take a holistic approach and target a wide set of factors.

Professional ethos (values and beliefs) serves to insulate our personnel from moral angst and provides the ethical certainty inherent in the immutable values of loyalty, duty, courage and integrity, which are demonstrably professed and practiced. Our ethos constitutes our 'moral compass' and our shield against ethical uncertainty. Yet, it is insufficient that the compass exists metaphorically as a technology. To influence his decision-making, the soldier must know the compass, understand it, be convinced of its value, know how to use it, use it properly, and trust it.

Leadership is an essential component in creating a coherent overall approach to fostering ethical behavior in an organization as the effects of leadership are often more profound than those of other ethical tools, such as codes of conduct. This includes both leadership through direction from superiors to those under their supervision; and leadership by example, whereby seniors 'practice what they preach'. By extension, where ethical leadership lacks competency, it can lead to sub-standard practice across the organization through misplaced advice, orders, or omissions.

Ethical Problems in an Age of Terror and Insurgency

The impact of global terrorism on the ethics of warfare is a subject of ongoing debate among policymakers, scholars, and thoughtful citizens. Should this novel threat alter the moral constraints ordinarily imposed on combatants, and if so, how and why? This challenge, along with the efforts of a seemingly increasing number of groups resorting to terrorism as apolitical strategy, has thrust the notion into the forefront of public consciousness. The notion of terrorism carries along with it a negative connotation and effectively labeling some violent acts as acts of terrorism, is a good way to raise doubts about the moral propriety of the act. Viewed from this perspective, championing the laws of warfare means all sorts of pain but no gain for the stronger side in an asymmetric conflict. Although many of the ethical problems typically appear to require trade-offs between moral values, it is often possible to reconcile these values when options are carefully considered and appropriate methods are leveraged.

Military ethics have come under scrutiny during global war on Terror. The question of what constitutes a just war and how it might be waged justly are highlighted in many countries actively engaged in counter-terrorist operations. How far can the ethical envelope be legitimately pushed before it stops protecting the country and causes irreparable harm to the things for which the country stands? In 2004, United Nations Security Council Resolution 1566, condemned terrorist acts as: 'criminal acts, including against civilians, committed with the intent to cause death or serious bodily injury, or taking of hostages, with the purpose to provoke a state of terror in the general public or in a group of persons or particular persons, intimidate a population or compel a government or an international organization to do or to abstain from doing any act, which constitute offences within the scope of and as defined in the international conventions and protocols relating to terrorism, are under no circumstances justifiable by considerations of a political, philosophical, ideological, racial, ethnic, religious or other similar nature'.[4] The key to a moral understanding of terrorism is that it consists in the use of force against those who should not have force used against them. With the above criterion in mind a moral definition of terrorism could be:

'terrorism is the deliberate, negligent, or reckless use of force against non-combatants, by state or non-state actors for ideological ends and in the absence of a substantial just legal process'. [5]

We need to reflect on how terrorism presents a profound moral and legal challenge for the military. It raises the myriad of questions: Is terrorism committed by non-state actors nonetheless an act of war? Do ordinary rules of war, which seek to protect civilians as much as possible from violence, apply? Is the distinction between combatants and civilians still viable in an age of terrorism? What legal and ethical constraints on military responses to terrorism should we advocate and why? Discussions range from suicide bombing and state-sponsored assassination to the individual versus collective morality, the evolution of the concept of jihad in Islam since the early years of the Prophet Mohammad, and the question of when, if ever, torture is justified. The terrorists, the jihadis, or the suicide bombers sometimes employ female and children, thus, making full use of the liberties available in democracy. They try to destroy the very basics of the nation state. Whilst operating against them, the armed forces distinguish between civilians and non-civilians. A terrorist does not. They will systematically leverage our compliance with general rules of war or rules of engagement, Geneva Convention, democratic norms and human rights into an advantage for their side without complying with any one of them.

Insurgency is an asymmetric conflict driven by a philosophy that seriously undermines human needs and aspirations. Such warfare besides impinging on the conventional war fighting capabilities of the militaries, also, imposes on them restrictive rules of engagement, in a battle space marked by a very high degree of unconventionality, uncertainty, and irrationality. Today, almost all insurgency movements are witnessing a very high profile of terrorist activity that aims to cause anarchy, paralysis, and disorder and helps the perpetrators to shape the asymmetric battle space.[6] The key is that, unlike a terrorist, an insurgent is completely reliant upon the population, and the population is the objective for both the insurgent and the counter-insurgent. Understanding cultural asymmetries helps in identifying and preparing for such asymmetric threats, as one has a better understanding of the enemy's capabilities and motives. Such operations demand that all military operations are people-centric and conducted in a manner that generates a groundswell for peace and creates redundancy of terrorists and insurgents in the environment. Hence, the rules of engagement have to be formulated imaginatively, in the backdrop of political, legal, and moral parameters.

Ethical Dilemmas in Asymmetrical Warfare

We face an enemy in the war on terror that neither observes the fundamental rules of international humanitarian law, nor respects the code of the warrior's honor. We face a terrorist strategy in which casualties, civilian and non-combatant are intrinsic to their object of war. The ethical command dilemma is how we remain true to a warrior code of honor that the enemy does not share; or how do we observe ethical restraint when the other side will not? The tactical and operational dilemma we may face is that our opponents could come to believe that they gain an advantage in breaking the Laws of War by engaging in perfidy, subterfuge, and a blatant disregard for human life - yours, theirs, and everyone else's. Yet Services can only prosper and retain their legitimacy, self-respect, confidence, and public support through Laws of War restraint, and by refusing to stain their warrior honor.

As a commander, one may face five unique moral dilemmas:[7]

- **Moral numbing**—The ethical implications of stand-off weapon systems generating hubris in technical performance that may mask reality, by making us forget or become numb to the fact that we are killing.
- **Moral frustration**—The temptation of vengeance, revenge, or the gratuitous use of force against those who display no warrior's honor, who have defiled our comrades, and who degrade their claim to combatant respect.
- **Perverse consequences of doing good**—The more ethnically pure our conduct is, the more likely this observance may be exploited by the enemy as a potential weakness or vulnerability. This includes the inseparable dilemma of hostage taking, the use of human shields, or the siting of enemy military objectives near hospitals and schools.
- **Perverse consequences in risk aversion. Casualty avoidance is a primary concern in our military culture**—We face an enemy who is prepared to die, not in the cause of victory, but simply as a contribution to perpetual conflict. With no hope of tactical victory, they choose martyrdom in a

vainglorious but failing attempt to make us look weak, inept, and unprepared.

- **The legalization of ethical reasoning**—While acting in accordance with the laws of the land is deemed to be ethical, societal values hold the Indian soldier to the highest possible ethical standards. Therefore, fidelity in maintaining the expectation of public trust is an operational imperative. Operational ethics is a command responsibility. The Laws of War help, and do not hinder, the conduct of operations. It is important that the letter and spirit of each tenet of international law be thoroughly understood so that neither the success of the mission nor the welfare of the soldier is compromised.

The strength of our Army in meeting the complexity, ambiguity, and ethical uncertainty of asymmetrical operations rest in our uncompromising adherence to an *Army ethos* (our values and beliefs) based on our expectations of army service, army values, and the societal expectations. Operational success demands qualities such as emotional intelligence, empathy, subtlety, sophistication, nuance, and political adroitness. An ethical warrior is a more skilful and adaptive warrior. Put simply, an ethical warrior reflects empathy when empathy works and lethal aggression when such is required.

Zero tolerance for ethical failings should not be confused with a "zero defects" mentality. Notwithstanding our best intentions, the fog of war makes operational mistakes or miscalculations inevitable. There is a clear distinction between making a mistake and doing wrong. A mistake is simply a judgment leading to an undesirable result, while doing wrong is an individual choice that violates our integrity. Mistakes illustrate important lessons from which we learn, and serve to test the fidelity of our trust in our subordinates and command.

Morality of War –Combating Terrorism and Insurgency

The national thrust in any counter-insurgency campaign would usually involve a four- pronged approach which would include:

- Creation of a secure environment in which the military will have a major role to play. The fundamental operational dilemma is rooted in the issue of terrorist identity.
- Prevention of any external support to the terrorists as has been seen in our case, in the form of moral, financial, material, and even personnel assistance.
- Own political and governmental institutions to address local aspirations.
- Perception management of all state and non-state stakeholders in the domestic, regional, and international environment through well conceived information operations.

The Terrorists, beyond doubt are the most critical element of any asymmetric environment as they introduce asymmetry into the environment through an irrational, indiscriminate, unpredictable, and ruthlessly destructive modus operandi.[8] Knowing their characteristics, capabilities, sources of power from which they derive freedom of action, physical strength, or the will to fight are, therefore, sine-qua-non. Motivations for indulging in such activities could range from a desire for some livelihood owing to intolerable poverty stricken conditions, to compensation for low esteem status, to religion/or ideology driven needs, to vendetta driven needs, wherein affected people want 'right the wrongs' with force.

National military forces throughout the world today

are involved in combating terrorist and insurgent activities. As various headquarters and agencies examine and tackle the problems, it is a very troubling issue for all. We must consider not only what we can do, but also what we ought to do. Some measures that might be highly effective will also be highly questionable from a legal or moral point of view. Acts of terrorism by non-state participants would require a new theory and invite a fresh way of thinking about when and how armed force can be justifiably employed. Asymmetric warfare operations put the maximum strain on the soldiers' professional ethics. There are pragmatic reasons for ethical restraint. We operate under intense media glare. Close scrutiny will come from our own society. We also have to win hearts and mind of people. We have to destroy the legitimacy of such opponents.

As against conventional operations, operations fought in the lower end of the 'Spectrum of conflict', entail application of combat power to enhance the 'civil control' in an affected area rather than cause 'destruction'. It is the use of minimum force by the security forces to create a secure and conducive environment so that root causes of the conflict can be addressed, in line with the nation's policy and strategy. Whilst it is necessary to have a humane approach towards the populace in the conflict zone, it would also be expected that overwhelming force is applied against foreign terrorists and hardcore inimical elements, while affording full opportunity to indigenous misguided elements to shun violence and join the mainstream. It underscores scrupulous respect for Human Rights, upholding laws of the land and encouraging 'neutralization' of terrorists by seeking surrenders and apprehensions rather than only seeking 'kills'.

India is possibly the only country in the world that has faced insurgencies and terrorism of all kinds-ethnic, ideological and ethno-religious for over 60 years. Yet, despite this sustained onslaught on its very being, India has survived this. After 67 years of independence, India and Pakistan the main perpetrator of terrorism in India, are on different trajectories.[9] Battling terror is a long and arduous task: the capability to prevent attacks has to be upgraded constantly, with the knowledge and acceptance that not all can be prevented. It is a hard battle where there are no rules for the terrorists and no scruples. Democracies have their inhibitions. Terrorism can never be overcome through good intentions. It will be overcome or managed through exercising hard options. This new form of struggle is an attempt on the part of terrorist groups to erase two basic features of war: the front and the uniform. These militants and terrorists fight without military uniforms, in ordinary and indistinguishable civilian garb, taking shelter among the civilian population; and they attack besides security forces, unarmed civilians wherever they are, intentionally and indiscriminately. Moreover, fighting an enemy who does not abide by the laws of warfare is morally ambiguous, and the resulting stress is enormous.

We have also seen on number of occasions, militants embedded in the civilian population did not carry weapons while moving from one position to another. Arms and ammunition had been pre-positioned for them and stored in different houses. By disguising themselves as civilians and by attacking civilians with no uniforms and with no front, these terrorist organizations attempt nothing less than to erase the distinction between combatants and non-combatants on both sides of the struggle. Suicide bombers exploded themselves on buses, in restaurants and in crowded market places.

The Indian Armed Forces and other Security Forces are engaged in combating such militants day in and day out while exercising maximum restraint in the conduct of such operations. An ethical code of conduct governing accession to and behavior of troops engaged in these tasks have been articulated and salient features of these among other things include No Rape, No Molestation, No Torture, No Meddling in Civil Administration, Respect Human Rights, etc.[10] Besides, extensive guidelines have been laid down for the conduct of counter-insurgency operations keeping in mind the legal framework and the existing insurgency environment. Security forces deployed in such areas are also briefed about human rights violations. The aim of the Indian Army's ethics code is to strike a coherent and morally plausible position that provides our security personnel effective tools to protect our citizens and win the war whilst also setting the proper moral limits that have to be met while legitimately securing our citizens.

It would be also appreciated that any overreaction also leads to the shattering of our moral legitimacy in this struggle. In a democratic society with a citizen's army, any erosion of the ethical foundation of its soldiers and its citizens is of immense political and strategic consequence. Ensuring ethical certainty within the asymmetrical battle space and developing our moral center demands a healthy ethical climate, free from reprisal, which inspires the moral courage to 'speak truth to power' in fixing the problem and not the blame.

Permissions and Restrictions in the Use of Force

The end state sought by military operations is a secure environment that will allow other elements of national power to function without hostile disruptions. To attain a secure environment, it is important to neutralize inimical elements in the area of operations that would normally disrupt or retard the peace initiatives as a part of the national strategy. Military has a lead role to play in accomplishing this task of creating a secure environment. A secure environment would be characterized by the return to a normal way of life, wherein civil liberties get fully restored and people are able to pursue their life styles with freedom, respect, human dignity far removed from the fear of the terrorist's gun.

Nothing captures the difficulties that combating irregular threats places on the military ethic better than the recent controversy surrounding the rules of engagement (ROE). While these rules correctly recognize the importance of minimizing risk to non-combatants, they often increase the risk to soldiers and, by extension, mission accomplishment. Despite the fact that our strikes against insurgent positions are almost always proportionate and discriminate, insurgents are often able to portray their casualties as civilian casualties. Insurgents, thus portray not only their own casualties, but also the civilian casualties the insurgents themselves cause as a result of security forces operations.

What the examples in the field show is that there is an inherent tension between the imperatives of accomplishing missions, protecting the force, and minimizing harm to non-combatants that often makes finding ethically permissible courses of action difficult. Further, these examples suggest that finding such courses of action requires assessing where to accept risk; they also suggest that where one should accept risk is situation-dependent. This means that general rules meant to cover a wide range of situations will be difficult, if not impossible, to establish. Rather, ethical behavior against irregular adversaries will be somewhat ad-hoc, that is, it will require individual soldiers and their leaders to be sensitive to local conditions at the time and the particulars of their mission, their organization, and the civilians in their area of operations.

The rules of war entail balancing three competing imperatives: accomplishing the mission, protecting the force, and minimizing harm. Determining that balance entails determining where one should accept risk. Accomplishing mission puts soldiers and noncombatants at risk; protecting the force puts mission accomplishment and noncombatants at risk; and minimizing harm puts mission accomplishment and force protection at risk. Where risk should be assigned depends on the ends the use of military force is intended to achieve. What those ends are depends on the character of the adversary.[11]

Concurrent conduct of perception management is also an operational imperative and must be imaginatively undertaken as part of the public information drive which hinges on effective dissemination of information through the watchful eyes of media both print and electronic. The aim is to keep the target audience informed in a manner that enables effective conflict management and creates necessary environment for its resolution.

Human Rights And Asymmetrical Warfare

Human Rights, both conceptually and practically, are not new. The basic principles can be found in all religious traditions, ancient and modern as well as in all philosophical traditions. In India, the traditional application of humanitarian law to the armed forces is almost as old as the armed conflicts themselves. There are several examples of prescribed humane behavior for the forces during conflict in Ramayana and Mahabharata. These are part of our cultural legacy. Lord Krishna taught Arjun and his soldiers about righteousness or '*Dharma*'. Guru Gobind Singh, a warrior, poet, philosopher, tenth of ten Sikh Gurus, in his invocation to the Almighty *'Deh Shiva bar mohe ihai. Shubh Karman Te kabhu Na taro, Na daroo ar siyoo jab jah karoon. Nischal kar apni jeet karoo' (O Lord, give me this boon. May I never shirk from doing good deeds. Never may I fear when I go to the enemy. With surety victory will be mine)* best exemplifies his call to the Khalsa brotherhood to be ready to sacrifice at the call of *Dharma*.[12]

The institutional culture of the Indian Army in counter-insurgency/low intensity conflict has evolved from its extensive experiences in the NE, Punjab, Sri Lanka and J&K. The counter-insurgency culture of the Indian Army is characterized by a focus on operational effectiveness that is aimed at blunting the instruments of violence to facilitate a political process.[13] The concept of '*Iron Fist* with *Velvet Glove*' followed by the Indian Army best exemplifies its humane approach towards the populace at large in the conflict zone. A people friendly approach while making the environment secure would contribute in ensuring smooth and effective functioning of government institutions.

Human rights are relevant to terrorism as it concerns both its victims and its perpetrators. The concept of human rights was first expressed in the 1948 Universal Declaration of Human Rights, which established 'recognition of the inherent dignity and inalienable rights of all members of the human family.' The innocent victims of terrorism suffer an attack on their most basic right to live in peace and security. The suspected perpetrators of attacks also have rights, as members of the human family, in the course of their apprehension and prosecution. They have the right not to be subject to torture or other degrading treatment, the right to be presumed innocent until they are deemed guilty of the crime, and the right to public trial.

Genuine respect for rights would mean that an existing legal system recognizes the rights in question and effectively upholds the respect for them. Of course this does not mean that violations never occur; no legal system can secure perfect compliance with its norms. It means that violations are on the whole prevented by adequate education, socialization, and police protection and those who commit such violations are apprehended and dealt with, to a sufficient degree to make respect for the human rights in question high. Also mechanisms for ensuring scrupulous respect for human rights must stay focused to preclude terrorists' and insurgents' machinations at maligning security forces through contrived situations and manipulated incidents. Over the years, the media has become increasingly active in highlighting actual or perceived human rights violations. As a result, even authorized population control measures undertaken by troops get projected as human rights violations.

Conclusion

As the Indian armed forces are engaged in the resolution of the ongoing insurgencies in J&K and NE, the possibility of prevalent socio-economic facets being exploited by inimical elements to vitiate the internal security environment cannot be ruled out. The armed and other security forces find themselves embroiled in complex counter-insurgencies and counter-terrorist campaigns where identifying the enemy, as well as identifying the best means to defeat him, is filled with uncertainty. This practical uncertainty entails ethical uncertainty as well: it is impossible to know what the rules of the game are if one does not know what game is in play. Otto von Bismarck's, (a Prussian and German statesman of the 19th century) statement that the 'the strong is weak because of his moral scruples and the weak grows strong because of his audacity', reflects the cultural asymmetry of values, norms, and rules.

A nation that fights such a war places many assets at risk: population, land, and interests. A non-state actor's or an insurgent's only asset is his idea. He may have interests and he probably has a target population. The goal of the players on both sides of an asymmetric war, as in counter-insurgency, is to win over the population to support their side-only then the enemy grows weak. If an asymmetric enemy has interests, then these interests must be targeted as well. No atrocity is beyond this enemy's capability.

Central to countering the proxy war and insurgency in the state of Jammu and Kashmir, and NE has been the campaign to *'Win the Hearts and Minds' (WHAM)*.While people are the main focus and winning the hearts and minds is the core strategy in counter-militancy, implementing the same is a challenge. Given that *WHAM* entails addressing varied issues such as identity, culture, language, religion, and human rights, evolving a holistic policy require an in-depth understanding of the core issues of militancy. A calibrated use of force concomitantly ensuring security and rights of people, addressing their latent socio-political aspirations and economic needs will pave the way for a clearly delineated strategy of *WHAM*.[14] We cannot fight a war against terror and hope to win if we betray our own moral high ground. It is about holding together the moral identity of the command that we exercise. Apart from few errors of judgment that occur in the heat of the moment which result from spontaneous reactions and may be avoidable, all deliberate acts of human rights violations can be curbed and must be ruthlessly dealt with.

The 'war on terror' has brought human rights issues into sharper focus. The rapid developments of more stringent counter-terrorism and counter-insurgency efforts have pitched the issue of human rights into high relief. Human rights, however, cannot be considered a zero-sum game. In the long term, an insistence that all states prioritize human rights and prosecute illegitimate violence will be the best defense against terrorism and insurgency. This mandates commanders at all levels to expeditiously investigate alleged human rights violations to mete out speedy justice. The fundamental stance of the Armed forces entailing 'Zero Tolerance' must be reiterated to one and all from time to time. With the involvement of the armed forces in such conflicts having become a permanent feature, adherence to the Laws of Armed Conflict and Human Rights, thus, assumes greater significance.

The track record of Indian Armed Forces in following human rights is second to none. In fact , there is no parallel instance where a country, facing proxy war and intense insurgency situations, aided and abetted by a foreign power, and where its security forces have suffered such heavy losses, has maintained such a disciplinary code. Terrorism today is a hydra-like monster. Its primary targets are liberal and democratic societies. It is a threat, which requires a multiple track response: political, diplomatic, military, policing, and law and order to name a few. In the absence of a global framework, domestic legislations remain the only legal remedy against terrorism.[15]

References

1. '*Asymmetric Warfare*' Wikipedia, The Free Encyclopedia.
2. Col Kulbhushan Bhardwaj-'The Theory of Asymmetry and its Practice in the Indian Sub-continent' in '*The War College Journal*-Winter 2013', pp36-44.
3. 'Facilitating Professional character development using Stories, Vignettes and case Studies, Chapter IV-Ethics Battlespace', at Center for the Army Profession and Ethic, 30 Sep 2013.
4. en.wikipedia.org/wiki/Definitions of Terrorism
5. "Terrorism without Intention" by David Rodin, pp177-185, in the book '*The Morality of War-A Reader*', edited by David Kinsella &Craig. Carr-VIVA Book Private Limited.
6. Christopher C. Harman-'*Terrorism Today*' -London Frank Cass, 2001, p53.

7. "*Duty with Discernment-CLS Guidance on Ethics in Operations,* Part A - Command Authority (Officers): Ensuring ethical certainty and moral resilience" - 2009, pp 7-14.

8. Paul Wilikinson-'*Political Terrorism*'-New York John Wiley & Sons, 1974, p17.

9. "Terrorism in India: External Ramifications" by Vikram Sood, pp121-131, *CLAWS Journal,* Summer 2009.

10. Vivek Chadha in "Role of Morals, Ethics and Motivation in a Counter -insurgency environment", 2013, Institute for Defence Studies and Analysis, *Journal of Defence Studies,* Vol 7,No2, April-June 2013, pp49-68.

11. Tony Plaff -'Resolving Ethical Challenges in an era of Persistent Conflict' at *http://www.Strategic* Studies Institute.army.mil.

12. Gen V.P.Malik-'Human Rights in the Armed Forces' at www.observerindia.com.

13. Maj Gen (now Lt Gen- since retd) Prakash Menon, PVSM, VSM, former GOC CI Force (V) in his talk on 'Problems faced in implementation of Human Rights and views on applicability of Laws of Armed Conflict in LICO' at the Army management Studies Board sponsored Seminar on "Laws of Armed Conflict &Human Rights-Perspectives and Challenges", 21-22 March 2006 at Bangalore.

14. *CLAWS* Manekshaw Paper No 14 of 2009-"Winning the Hearts and Minds-Lessons from Jammu and Kashmir" by Brig Rahul K. Bhonsle(retd).

15. Concluding remarks by Gen V.P. Malik(Retd). Former COAS, in his essay titled "Human Rights in the Armed Forces" at www.observerindia.com.

7

The Art of Ethical Decision Making*

"Every time you make a serious moral judgment, you become that judgment; every time you issue a command, you not only tell your subordinates what to do but what to be. That is why, in the horrible circumstances in which you or your soldiers might find yourselves in the months ahead in a world seemingly gone morally mad, I trust in you because of the moral compass which is yours from your education, your experience, your expertise. You do on the basis of your information; you are on the basis of your formation. Ethics, in the final analysis, is caught, not taught."

Toner, James H. "Leading Soldiers in Moral Mayhem. - In the future of the Army Profession".

(*Extracts of the essay published in 'TRISHUL-The Tri-Service Professional Journal ,DSSC', Wellington, Autumn 2012, pp 25-36.)

Introduction

Leadership requires moral courage and a sense of how a decision in good conscience might be structured. As unskilled ethical decision makers, we can end up shaving off pieces of ourselves in order to live with ethical compromises. But as skillful decision makers, we can embrace our full selves and live simpler, more satisfying lives. We all have an image of our better selves, of how we are when we act ethically or are 'at our best.' We probably also have an image of what an ethical community, an ethical business/profession, an ethical government, or an ethical society should be. Ethics really has to do with all these levels, acting ethically as individuals, as professionals, creating ethical organizations and governments, and making our society as a whole ethical in the way it treats everyone.

We in the Services pride ourselves on being a 'Value based' institution with the admonition in its doctrine to 'do what's right'. In our leadership manual it has been stressed that character helps one to know what is right; more than that it links knowledge to action. Character encompassing a leader's moral and ethical qualities helps determine what is right and gives a commander motivation to do what is appropriate.[1]

What is Ethics?

Study of ethics encompasses virtues of character. Simply stated, ethics refers to standards of behavior that tell us how human beings ought to act in the many situations in which they find themselves-as friends, parents, children, citizens, business people, teachers, professionals, and so on. Values determine what is right and what is wrong, and doing what is right or wrong is what we mean by ethics. To behave ethically is to behave in a manner consistent with what is right or moral.[2] It is helpful to identify *what ethics is NOT*:

Ethics is not the same as feelings.

Feelings provide important information for our ethical choices. Some people have highly developed habits that make them feel bad when they do something wrong, but many people feel good even though they do something wrong. And often our feelings will tell us it is uncomfortable to do the right thing if it is hard.

Ethics is not religion.

Many people are not religious, but ethics applies to everyone. Most religions do advocate high ethical standards but sometimes do not address all the types of problems we face.

Ethics is not following the law.

A good system of law does incorporate many ethical standards, but law can deviate from what is ethical. Law can become ethically corrupt, as some totalitarian regimes have made it. Law can be a function of power alone and designed to serve the interests of narrow groups. Law may have a difficult time designing or enforcing standards in some important areas, and may be slow to address new problems.

Ethics is not following culturally accepted norms.

Some cultures are quite ethical, but others become corrupt or blind to certain ethical concerns (as the United States was to slavery before the Civil War). 'When in Rome, do as the Romans do' is not a satisfactory ethical standard.

Ethics is not science.

Social and natural science can provide important data to help us make better ethical choices. But science alone does not tell us what we ought to do. Science may provide an explanation for what humans are like. But ethics provides reasons for how humans ought to act. And just because something is scientifically or technologically possible, it may not be ethical to do it.

Leader and His Role in Ethical Decision Making

Making choices is at the heart of ethics. Ethics presupposes choice, and choice pre-supposes at least some measure of freedom. As an organized discipline, ethics emphasizes systematically finding the best choices for making particular choices or crafting certain policies. It can be thought of as a guide to using one's freedom to choose. Studying ethics helps distinguish between better and worse reasons behind particular courses of action and to choose the most reasonable path in the light of values of that organization. Military ethics applies to a specialized realm and has developed principles appropriate to it over time to help guide future practices.

Leaders become credible and authentic as ethical role models by engaging in ongoing behaviors that subordinates deem unselfish and ethically appropriate. These behaviors include being honest, showing consideration for others, treating people fairly and with respect and taking ethically correct decisions. By doing so, leaders set an example for others to identify and imitate them. This is an ongoing process; subordinates are continuously evaluating their leaders, so a leader, who is ethical at one point in time and not at another, sends, mixed messages that damage his authenticity.

Making good ethical decisions requires a trained sensitivity to ethical issues and a practiced method for exploring the ethical aspects of a decision and weighing the considerations that should impact our choice of a course of action. Having a method for ethical decision making is absolutely essential. When practiced regularly, the method becomes so familiar that we work through it automatically without consulting the specific steps. The more novel and difficult the ethical choice we face, the more we need to rely on discussion and dialogue with others about the dilemma. Only by careful exploration of the problem, aided by the insights and different perspectives of others, can we make good ethical choices in such situations.

Ethics in Practice

An ethical dilemma is a complex situation that will often involve an apparent mental conflict between moral imperatives, in which to obey one would result in transgressing another. Ethical dilemmas are often cited in an attempt to refute an ethical system or moral code, as well as the worldview that encompasses or grows from it. At these times, we are caught in a conflict between right and right. And no matter what option we choose, we feel like we have come up short. Ethical compromises, big or small, dull our sense of where to draw the line. They instill a habit of distorted thinking and put us at risk of losing control of our decisions. Critical thinking is the coin of the ethicist's realm.[3]

Making ethical decisions is easy when the facts are clear and the choices black and white. But it is a different story when the situation is clouded by ambiguity, incomplete information, multiple points of view, and conflicting responsibilities. In such situations, leaders experience, all the time-ethical decisions depend on both the decision making process itself and on the experience, intelligence, and integrity of the decision maker.[4] Many cases of misconduct, cheating, misappropriation, bribery, though may appear different but they have a lot in common since they are full of the oldest questions in the world - questions of human behavior and human judgment applied in ordinary day-to-day situations. We have to ask how usually honest, intelligent, compassionate human beings could act in ways that are callous, dishonest, and wrongheaded. Very often the explanations for such acts go back to four rationalizations/beliefs that people have relied on through the ages to justify questionable conduct as mentioned here: [5]

- **A belief that activity is within reasonable ethical and legal limits**—A belief that the activity is not 'really' illegal or immoral. The idea that an action is not really wrong is an old issue. How far is too far? Exactly where is the line between a smart and too smart? Between sharp and shady? Put enough people in an ambiguous, ill defined situation and some will conclude that whatever has not been labeled specifically wrong must be all right, especially if they are rewarded for certain acts. Seniors seldom ask their subordinates to do things that both of them know, are against the law or impudent. But often they leave things unsaid or give the impression that there are things they don't want to know about. In other words, they can seem, whether deliberately or otherwise, to be distancing themselves from their subordinate's tactical decisions in order to keep their own hands clean, if things go awry. Often such people lure ambitious subordinates by implying that rich rewards await those who can produce certain results and that the methods for achieving them will not be scrutinized too closely.
- **A belief that the activity is in the individual's or the organization's best interests**—This implies that the individual would somehow be expected to undertake the activity. This nearly always results from a parochial view of what those interests are.

Ambitious people look for ways to attract favorable attention, something to distinguish from other people. So they try to outperform their peers. Some may see that it is not difficult to look remarkably good in the short run by avoiding things that pay off only in the long run. The sad truth is that many such people have been promoted on the basis of 'great' results obtained in just those ways, leaving unfortunate successors to inherit the inevitable consequences.

- **A belief that the activity is 'safe' because it will never be found out or publicized**—This is the classic crime-and-punishment issue of discovery. It is perhaps the most difficult to deal with because it is often true. A great deal of proscribed behavior escapes detection. Also, we know that conscience alone does not deter everyone. How can we deter wrong doing that is unlikely to be detected? The most effective deterrent is not to merely increase the severity of punishment for those caught but to heighten the perceived probability of being caught in the first place. Here, especially in matters related financial dealings etc; by simply increasing the frequency of audit and spot checks is a deterrent, when combined with three other simple techniques: scheduling audits irregularly, making at least half of them unannounced, and setting up some checkups soon after others. A common error that most of us succumb to is to assume that because frequent audits uncover little behavior that is out of line, less frequent, and therefore less costly auditing is sufficient. But this opinion overlooks the important and deterrent effect of frequent checking. The point is to prevent misconduct not just to catch it. A trespass detected should not be dealt with discreetly.

- A belief that because the activity helps the organization, the establishment will condone it and even protect the person who engages in it. The question we have to deal with here is, how do we keep our loyalty from going berserk? Here, it is the seniors in the establishment who have the responsibility to exert a moral force within their own establishment or set-up. They need to draw the line between loyalty to their set-up against the laws and values of the service and the society in which we always operate. Further, because that line can be blurred in the heat of the moment, the line has to be drawn well short of where reasonable men and women could begin to suspect that their rights had been violated. The establishment has to react long before for an enquiry is ordered, and the prosecution has a strong enough case for indictment. Finally, most important of all, leaders must stress the excuses of organization loyalty, etc, will not be accepted for acts that place its good name in jeopardy.

Draw Distinctions- Overcoming Faulty Thinking

To assess the ethics of any action, it is useful to separate three dimensions of the action: *prudential, legal,* and *ethical.* Within the prudential dimension, we distinguish between what is prudent or not prudent; within the legal dimension, between what is lawful or unlawful; and within ethical dimension, between what is right or wrong. Ethically sensitive situations are often confounded by prudential and legal issues we fail to see. An action raises questions in the '*ethical*' dimension when it pertains to our pre-determined standards of right behavior. An action in accord with our code of behavior is obviously ethical, and when in conflict, unethical. Often principal issues in the ethical dimension are lying, deceiving, stealing, and causing harm. In moral philosophy, the general ability to make sound judgments is called '*prudence*' or *practical wisdom,* and it involves knowing both what goals are worth pursuing and what means will be most likely to achieve those goals. Furthermore, each professional area has its own specific prudence (such as medical prudence or military prudence). We can usually tell we are dealing with prudential dimension when we balance one issue with another, trade off plusses and minuses, and weigh opposing risks, to decide what the 'smart' thing to do is.

Figure-2, Draw Distinctions

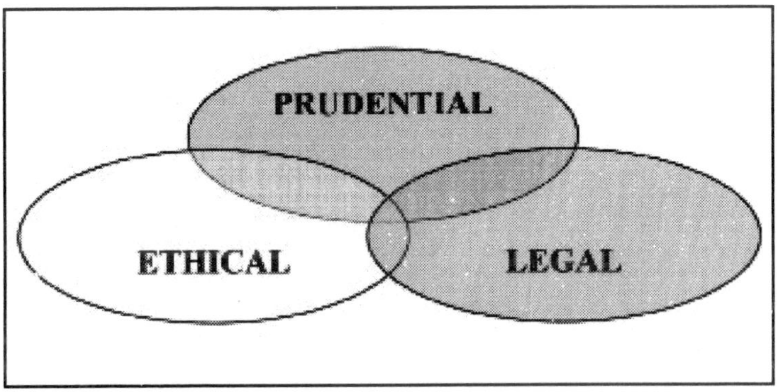

An action raises questions in the legal dimension it pertains to the law in the prevailing social system. Illegal acts obviously include prohibitions such as committing assault, speeding, murder, and possessing banned drugs etc. The law has a coercive aspect: if we break it, society condones physical force or threat of force against us or property.

We often fail to distinguish the three dimensions of an action, and thus, confuse and complicate decisions. When we become practiced at drawing the distinction between prudential, legal, and ethical dimensions of decisions, we notice something surprising: we encounter ethical dilemmas -situations in which two ethical principles conflict

- only rarely. With practice we can avoid creating false dilemmas and instead become more skilled at peeling away the prudential and legal issues to focus on just the ethical dilemmas and making more skillful ethical decisions.[6]

Ethical Dilemmas

The word dilemma comes from two Greek roots: di (double) and lemma (propositions). Therefore, a dilemma is a predicament in which the decision-maker must choose between two options of near or equal value. In addition, the dilemmas which confront modern professionals may result from options, which are not well defined, or from solutions, which create additional problems and harm for the problem carrier or for others. Ethical compromises erect social and emotional barriers between people --barriers that are stubborn and are hard to discuss. Tainted character is bad enough; strained relationships can be worse. Ethical compromise creates both. Our compromises undermine our sense of integrity.

We have all experienced, at one time or another, situations in which our professional responsibilities unexpectedly come into conflict with our deepest values. While invariably everyone manages to find some solution to their ethical problem, in the Services, the quality of the solution so found assumes special importance since it could affect the very fabric of the organization and more, the society itself. The moral consequences of our acts are too high for us to be cavalier about our moral performance. Here two very apt situations namely the concept of 'Moral Free Space' and 'Defining Moments' need to be highlighted.

Moral Free Space

Many activities are neither good nor bad but exist in 'moral free space'. As Einstein is reported to have said 'things should be as simple as possible, but not simpler.' Many practices that are considered un-ethical in one setting may be ethical in another. Such activities are neither black nor white but they exist in what one may call as 'moral free space'. In this grey zone, there are no tight prescriptions for one's behavior. We must chart our own course as long as we do not violate core human values. How can we discover the limits of this moral free space? That is, how can we learn to distinguish a value in tension with our own from one that is intolerable? Developing good ethical judgment would require clarity about core values and codes of conduct.[7]

Defining Moments

An ethical decision typically involves choosing between two options: one we know to be right and another we know to be wrong. A defining moment, however, challenges us in a deeper way by asking us to choose between two or more ideals in which we deeply believe.[8] Such challenges rarely have a 'correct' response. Rather, they are situations created by circumstances that ask us to step forward and 'form, reveal and test ourselves'. We 'form' our character in defining moments because we commit to irreversible courses of action that shape our personal and professional identities. We 'reveal' something new about us to ourselves and others because such moments uncover something that had been hidden or crystallize something that had been only partially known. And we 'test' ourselves because we discover whether we will live up to our personal beliefs/ideals or only pay them lip service. Those who are most satisfied in resolving such issues are the ones who undertake a process of probing self-enquiry if possible in quiet seclusion. In such introspection, one is able to dig below the busy surface of daily life and refocus on one's core values and principles. This endeavor renews one's sense of purpose at work and act as a springboard for shrewd, pragmatic, politically astute action. By repeating this process throughout one's working life, one is able to craft an authentic and strong identity based on one's own, rather than on someone else's understanding of what is right. And in this way, one begins to make the transition to becoming ethically right leader. Judgment is an essential and integral element of an ethical person.

Ethical Decision–Its Characteristics

An ethical decision is:

- One that is related to a specific context; in the same situation, there may be professional ethics, educational ethics, and personal ethics and sometimes one or more of these may be in conflict.
- One that is best for the organization rather than for the leader; one that is not self-serving.
- One that is made in the open and is consistent with full disclosure.
- One that is more right than wrong, even though it relates to a grey area where there is really no right or wrong answer,
- One that is honest and based on facts yet is consistent with the spirit of rightness and fair play.
- One that is consistent with the values and principles for which the organization and the institution stand.
- One that will be the best for the organization in both the short and long term.
- One that can be supported and defended by one's peers and superiors.
- One that is made in good faith.

An Ethical Decision Making Framework

An ethical decision making framework identifies five domains namely[9]:

- **Moral Awareness** – It implies an acknowledgement of one's moral obligations to the Service as one seeks to distinguish right from wrong and to identify 'what's best'.
- **Moral Judgment** – It is informed by a desire to maximize good and minimize harm; a respect for rules and established conventions and a desire to treat others fairly keeping in mind rights and dignities of self and others.
- **Moral Intention** – It determines the right course of action by acting in good conscience and realizing what one does, is never morally careless. Mistakes may occur but these are not mistakes due to moral neglect, selfishness or cowardice.
- **Moral Action** – It signifies action with a moral purpose and good will. It is not an act to deceive or perpetuate a wrong. One must act as a force for 'goodness and rightness' and not be ashamed in acting in such a manner. And finally,
- **Moral Reflection** – It suggests one to Stop and Think. An unexamined life is not worth living.

Based on the above precepts, the ethical decision so arrived would imply:

- Framing decisions in broader terms than self-interest.
- Minimizing harm and maximizing the good that comes from a course of action.

- Balancing competing factors by logical reflection.
- Ensuring actions are prosecuted with moral courage and in good conscience.
- Accepting responsibility for one's actions

Set of Questions

More as a practical guide, a set of questions that one should ask oneself when examining an ethical decision is given below.[10] Reflections on these questions will ensure ethical deliberation. These include:

- Have you defined the problem accurately? Extensive fact gathering may diffuse the emotionalism of an issue. Actually moral decision is an informed decision. A decision that is based on blind or convenient ignorance is hardly defensible.
- How would you define the problem if you stood on the other side of the fence? The discomfort of the alternative definition is meant to prompt a disinclination to choose the expedient over the most responsible course of action.
- How did this situation occur in the first place? Enquiry into its history gives a clue to solving the dilemma.
- To whom and to what do you give your loyalties as a person and as a member of the organization?
- What is your intention in making this decision?
- How does intention compare with the likely results?
- Whom could your decision or action injure?
- Can you engage the affected parties in a discussion of the problem before you make a decision?

- Are you confident that your position will be valid over a period of time as it seems now?
- Could you disclose without qualm your decision or action to your Superior/Senior, your family, or society as a whole?
- What is the symbolic potential of your action if understood? If misunderstood?
- Under what conditions would you allow exceptions to your stand?

A decision which answers one or more of these questions need not necessarily be the right one, but a failure to comply with any of these stipulations is likely to prejudice the ethical integrity of a decision.

Conclusion

A frame work for ethical decision making has been suggested in the hope that it will be a useful method for exploring ethical dilemmas and identifying ethical courses of action. We come across many sources of ethical standards but it will be observed at the end; all the approaches gives us important information with which to determine what is ethical in a particular circumstance. And more often than not, different approaches do lead to similar answers.

A leader whose concepts of ethics are vague and whose principles of ethics are ill defined and possibly even vacillating and inconsistent, is in constant danger of yielding to expediency and even pursuing unethical practices; or worse, providing an undesirable environment, wherein his subordinates can make such decisions based solely on their own personal ethical principles, with no frame of reference from the top. Of course, a well defined personal code, however high in standards, does not by itself ensure ethical conduct. It is very well to recognize right from wrong and to have good intentions, but leadership requires the moral courage to act upon what we know to be right. Our ethics are completely within our control, and regardless of what the future holds, we must take responsibility for our ethics at the time we make decisions.[11]

As we begin the journey to more effective and ethical thinking, whether as individuals, leaders, or others, we may succumb to blurred reasoning. But we will finish with habits that allow us to draw bright ethical lines to consistently guide skillful ethical decision making. In ethics as in everything else, developing habits requires repetition and reinforcement. As the saying goes, practice makes perfect--or more accurately, perfect practice makes perfect. If we are to make the most of skillful ethical decision making, we must turn it into a habit.[12]

References

1. "Qualities of a Commander-Character", in '*Manual on Command*' – An ARTRAC publication-Apr 2012, pg 106.
2. "*Strategic Leadership and Decision Making*", Chapter 15-'Values and Ethics', National Defence University. (USA)
3. "An Overview of Applied Ethics for the Military-Defining Ethics" by Bill Rhodes in "*An Introduction to Military Ethics*", 1959, pg 3.
4. "Ethics in Practice" by Kenneth R. Andrews in "*Ethics in Practice: Managing the Moral Corporation*" (Harvard Business School Press, 1989.)
5. "Why good managers make bad ethical choices" by Saul W. Gellerman, *Harvard Business Review*, July-August 1986.
6. Chapter 2- 'Draw Distinctions' in "*Ethics for the Real*

world' by Ronald A. Howard & Clinton D. Korver pp 35-39, Harvard Business Press, 2008.

7. "Values in Transition" by Thomas Donaldson in *Harvard Business Review*-September-October 1996.
8. "The Discipline of Building Character" by Joseph L. Badrarcco, Jr, *Harvard Business Review* on Leadership, pp 80-113.
9. "*Royal Australian Navy Leadership Ethic* — Annex B-An ethical Decision Making Model", pp 87-92.
10. "Ethics without the Sermon" by Laura L.Nash in *Harvard Business Review,* November-December 1981.
11. *Ibid,* Chapter 5, 'Choose Action', p 109.
12. "Habits of Wisdom" in Epilogue- in "*Ethics for the Real world*" by Ronald A. Howard & Clinton D. Korver, pg 152, Harvard Business Press, 2008.

8

Army Values: Building Blocks for Leadership*

(*Based on a talk to the Gentleman Cadets undergoing Pre-commission training at the Cadets Training Wing (CTW) at the Military College of Electronics and Mechanical Engineering (MCEME), Secunderabad-18 Feb 2012.)

Preamble

At the outset, I would like to thank the Commandant MCEME and Commander Cadets Training Wing (CTW) for giving me this opportunity to be with you all and share a few thoughts on a subject which is very vital, as it shapes your long and successful journey in the Army. You are all here at the CTW after willingly embracing a profession, the profession of arms, a profession of noble calling, indeed unique among all other professions. Here at the CTW, we train Gentlemen Cadets to become part of a professionally competent commissioned officer corps of the Indian Army.

Depending upon duration of your stay, you will one day be commissioned from the portals of this great institution as commissioned officers in various Arms and Services of the Indian Army. An officer is basically a leader with a strong intellect, physical presence, professional competence, moral character, and one who is indeed a 'Role Model'. As a leader you should be able and willing to act decisively within the intent and purpose of superior leaders and in the best interests of the organization. You are to become leaders who will inspire and influence others to carry out missions entrusted to you.

I am convinced that knowledge of the issues I will be touching upon will surely help you all to be the ethical standard bearers, to model the ideal and to forge an atmosphere of trust and confidence, as you progress in your career in the Army.

I am happy to be in the midst of you, young gentlemen cadets, our budding leaders of tomorrow, though I must also confess that I am little jealous of you young gentlemen, for as I enter into the evening hours of my life, you all have so many wonderful years ahead as I had behind me. I get this awesome feeling that though I am old in age, I am young in spirits today in your midst. Yes, being here at the CTW as a part of your pre-commissioning training, I believe you made the right choice, and indeed are fortunate to have chosen this path. Because beyond the hardship, heartbreak, and the sacrifice - and they are very real - there is another side to military service. You have an extraordinary opportunity - not just to protect the lives of your fellow soldiers, but for missions and decisions that may change the course of history. You will be challenged to go outside your comfort zone and take a risk in every sense of the word. To expand what you thought you were capable of doing when it comes to leadership, friendship, responsibility, agility, selflessness, and above all, courage. And you will be doing all of this at an age, when many of your peers in the civilian streets are reading spreadsheets and making photocopies. You must always remember that we are in the profession of arms, predicated on 'the will to win'. The sure knowledge that in war there is no substitute for victory and that if you fail the nation will be destroyed. Other than the officer corps, there is no group within our society toward which the obligation to the nation is more fully expressed.

Officership is not only leadership but also commandership, to order actions, persuade or compel execution, and evolve plans to achieve success and goals using soldiers, material, and ideas. So when we say soldiering or soldier, it is about the inseparable mix of soldier, his leader, officer, and commander. It is indeed an unique fascinating mix.

I will be covering the following aspects in my talk today:

- The Meaning of your commission
- Military ethos
- Values-Its Importance in the armed forces
- Core Values –Indian Army
- Importance of character

The Meaning of Your Commission

I have purposely begun this talk by mentioning this namely 'The meaning of your commission'. Yes, depending on the time you have already spent here and what you have to do at the CTW, you will all be joining the ranks as a commissioned officer of the Indian Army-- a journey providing you an access to a vigorous and exciting vista, our soldiers in their diverse shades and practices and soldiering in its multi-faceted form. You, as an officer are the *'steward of the future of the Army profession'*.

Upon being commissioned in the armed forces of our

country, a man incurs a lasting obligation to cherish and protect his country and to develop within himself that capacity and reserve strength, which will enable him to serve its arms and the welfare of his fellow Indians, with increasing wisdom, diligence, and patriotic conviction. Soldiers must be led and inspired by exemplary role models to become experts and assume the identity, character, and capabilities of a member of the profession.

This is the meaning of your commission. It is not modified by any reason of assignment while in the service, nor is the obligation lessened on the day an officer puts the uniform aside and returns to civil life. Having been specially chosen by the country to sustain the dignity and integrity of its sovereign power, an officer is expected to maintain himself, and to so exert his influence for as long as he may live, that he will be recognized as a worthy symbol of all that is best in the national character.

Please remember that the military profession is not a corporation or a business. *Military service is a calling*. Officers and soldiers do not stay in the military for monetary purposes only. They stay for the prestige of wearing the uniform and serving in a most honorable profession that requires dying as an ultimate sacrifice for service of the nation. Soldiers deserve inspired leadership from each one of you. Being an officer is more than holding a job and going home for dinner.

Yes, we are a profession committed to the 'unlimited and unrestrained' service to the nation, whenever and wherever our country calls. In our profession, even apparently mundane tasks take on extra-ordinary meaning. Our tasks apart from other things include military aid to civil community which includes helping the community in times of national disasters. Throughout our proud history, these tasks have always been part of our mission and they will always be.

Military Ethos

'Ethos' is a Greek word meaning 'character' that is used to describe the guiding beliefs or ideals that characterize a community, nation, or ideology. The armed forces of which each one of you are proud members provide a distinctive and important strand in the fabric of the nation. You are at the forefront of society in respecting and embracing diversity in every form. We promote the ideals of 'Leadership, Integrity, Discipline, Professionalism, Service, and Excellence'. Remember that it takes the combined effort and sacrifice of the total army to perform all its tasks as we deter the enemy.

Our way of life and our well being in the armed forces depends upon the ability of leaders at all levels to inspire and lead often under the most harrowing conditions and unimaginable levels of stress. How do we go about these duties is important question that props us. The Military ethos or its ethics has an important role to play here. The military officer is considered a gentleman, not because nation wills it, nor because it has been the custom of people in all times to afford him that courtesy, but specifically because nothing less than a gentleman is truly suited for his particular set of responsibilities.

The Military ethos encompasses values that describe professional conduct. This behavioral dimension of our effectiveness includes: the civic values of liberal democracy; values subsumed by the rule of law; ethical values governing our treatment of others and the conduct of operations; and the traditional military values of duty, loyalty, integrity, and courage. *The ethos is the essence of the warrior's honor.* It is intimately linked to leadership effectiveness.

Military ethos is central to our concepts of both the profession of arms and military leadership. The ethos of the Services ingrains in its personnel an unwavering will to succeed, accepting their grave responsibility and an unbridled ability to give their lives for others. They are confident that in return the nation will look after them and their families.

Values–its importance in the Armed Forces

You will agree with me that no discussion on military leadership would be complete without highlighting the pivotal role values play, their relevance and importance. Here, I shall touch upon some generic aspects only and later highlight the core values of Indian Army. The Concise Oxford Dictionary defines values as one's principles or standards; one's judgment of what is important in life. What emerges clearly is that:

- A value is a long standing belief upon which a person acts by preference.
- Each person develops certain guides to behavior which keeps giving direction to his life, e.g., a child who is brought up in an environment where the importance of helping others is emphasized will develop a positive attitude.
- An attitude is a behavioral readiness which gets built in as a result of holding on to certain values for long.
- Values may be regarded as the standards by which human beings are influenced in their choice amongst alternative courses of action.
- We draw from our values the purpose, direction, vitality and character-- the bedrock of all that we do in the armed forces.
- Values are necessary for regulating behavior and conduct of individual/group. They motivate us as

they keep us focused on why we are doing what we are doing and the ends towards which we are striving.

- They unite any establishment big or small around its purpose and vision.
- Values influence every aspect of our lives, our moral judgments, our responses to others, our commitments to personal and organizational goals.
- Values set parameters for our decisions and serve as guides to action.

Army values are more than a system of rules. They are not just a code tucked away in a drawer or a list in a dusty book. These values tell each one of us what we need to be, every day, in every action we perform. Army values form the very identity of the army, the solid rock upon which everything else stands, especially in combat. Army values are non-negotiable; they apply to everyone and in every situation throughout the army. They are the power that binds together the members of a noble profession. As a result, the whole is much greater than the sum of its parts. Army values remind the army members and tell the rest of the world, the civilian governments, the nation, even the enemy, what the Army stands for.

Let me first highlight the 'Ideal Military Values' from the organizational angle before I talk about 'Core Values of the Indian Army.'

Ideal Military Values (Organizational)

The aim of laying down military values is basically to emerge victorious in battle, always and every time, at minimum human cost. These are organizational demands on individuals which must be fulfilled. These include:

- **Obedience (to lawful command)**—It is the act of doing what one is told. It is dutifulness in an ambience of legitimacy. Remember loyalty and obedience are closely linked.
- **Individual and Collective Discipline**—Discipline is learning what to do, when to do it and in what manner it should be done. For the armed forces, discipline is the standard of personal deportment, work requirement, courtesy, appearance and ethical conduct, which will enable all to perform the mission with optimum efficiency. In fact, 'discipline is the soul of the army.'
- **Camaraderie**—It describes the feeling of belonging and concern for one another. It is a strong binding force which leads to lifelong friendships.
- **Regimental Spirit**—It is an indispensable condition for the Indian Army, a rallying point and source of inspiration.
- **Professional Competence (including keeping abreast with latest professional development)**—It makes you an officer of consequence. It is an officer's obligation and sacred duty to be professionally competent.
- **Subservience of personal interest to organizational interest**—Remember the *'Chetwode'* motto. It creates a sense of patriotism and nationalism and a very high level of officer-man relationship and bonding.
- **Secular profile**—Each officer irrespective of his caste, color, and creed is a soldier and that is the only religion followed by everyone. Clannish instincts based on religion, caste, etc have no place.
- **Apolitical**—It implies distancing from politicking and political involvement and allowing politics to

influence or interfere with professional conduct and discharge of duty. Despite India's increasing dependence on the Services to pull its chestnuts from fire time and again, the Services have scrupulously remained apolitical.

Core Values-Indian Army

Core values identified for the Indian Army are:

- NAM (HONOR)
- NAMAK (LOYALTY)
- NISHAN (ESPIRIT- DE- CORPS)
- VACHAN (COMMITMENT)
- COURAGE
- INTEGRITY
- SELFLESSNESS
- SELF- DISCIPLINE

Now I would like to spend some time in briefly highlighting what each of this mean/signify.

NAM (Honor)- Live up to all Army Values

Honor is the glue that holds the Army values together. Honor provides the 'moral compasses' for character and personal conduct in the Army. Though many people struggle to define the term, most recognize instinctively, those with a keen sense of right and wrong, those who live such that their words and deeds are above reproach. The term 'honorable person'; therefore, refers to both the character traits an individual actually possesses and the fact the community recognizes and respects them. For an army leader, honor means putting Army values above self-interest, above career and comfort. For all soldiers, it means putting army values above self-preservation as well. This honor is essential in creating a bond of trust among the members of the army and between the army and the nation.

The essentials of this Core value are:

- A fine and scrupulous sense of what is right and adherence to principles against all odds.
- A mental makeup which makes an officer rise above petty considerations and act as befits a leader of men and not just the mere acquisition of title, rank or privilege.

Honor embodies:

- Clean Conduct
- Incorruptibility
- Indomitable spirit
- Strong character with no compromise on principles
- High dedication and fair play
- Adherence to high personal values in the most trying conditions.

Namak (Loyalty)

Loyalty has to do with faithfulness, firmness in allegiance, and personal devotion in an ambience of legitimacy. Loyalty is built upon legitimacy and lawfulness, conforming to an accepted standard. Loyalty is to an idea, a person, a group, or an organization. This framework of loyalty-legitimacy must be clearly understood. Obedience is an act of doing what one is told; it is dutifulness. These nuances are important and as one grows in rank and responsibility, they attain greater meaning, relevance, and emphasis.

As a loyal individual you need to do the following:

- Respect the rules and regulations.
- Put obligations in correct order: the constitution, the army, the unit, and finally the self.
- Observe higher headquarters priorities.
- Work within the system without manipulating it for personal advantage.
- Show faithfulness to unit and comrades.
- Carry out tough orders without expressing personal criticism.
- Defend soldiers against unfair treatment from outside or above.

Nishan (Esprit-De-Corps)

Comradeship and regimental spirit add up to make 'Esprit-de-Corps', an essential element of high morale, a priceless asset, which costs much less than the most up-to-date weapons. But without it, the most sophisticated military hardware is of little value. Espirit-de-Corps, the powerful effect of group membership, is a major factor which promotes courageous behavior. The ethos, in which an individual is prepared to make any sacrifice for the good name and honor of the unit/regiment/corps, has been with us for centuries. The joint family system in our very homes has helped promote esprit-de-corps.

Our pride in our units and formation has been a major factor in exemplary performance of Indian Army since Independence. The regimental system has given our officers and men a sense of belonging and a cause bigger than themselves, and has acted as a crucible for promoting esprit-de-corps.

Vachan (Commitment)

When our value system is clear, it becomes a lot easier to make decisions and commitments. You cannot keep a friend by revealing to others what he told you in confidence. You cannot do justice to a job by trying to do as little as possible. When a person makes a commitment to someone, he is really saying, 'You can count on me no matter what', and 'I will be there'.

Commitment implies:

- I am willing to sacrifice.
- I am a person of integrity and you can trust me.
- I will not let you down.
- Despite pain, I will be there.

Commitment brings:

- Predictability
- Security
- Personal growth
- Strong relationships among officers and men
- Lasting personal and professional relationships

Courage

Courage is the ability to face danger, fear, or adversity (physical or moral) Bravery is instinctive, almost a mechanical reaction. Courage is a virtue, a lofty and noble sentiment. It takes two forms: Physical and Moral. Physical courage means overcoming fear of bodily harm and doing one's duty. Moral courage is the willingness to stand firm on values, principles and convictions, even when threatened. It enables leaders to stand up for what they believe is right, regardless of the consequences. Courageous leaders are willing to look critically inside themselves, consider new ideas, and change what needs changing. In combat, physical and moral courage may blend together. The right thing to do may not only be unpopular, but dangerous as well. Such situations reveal who is a leader of character and who is not. Cowardice, on the other hand, makes a person hide the truth; one who is courageous will not lie.

Courage is a studied, deliberate and determined counter attitude to danger and adversity; it is long lasting, and has a larger intellectual and moral content than physical courage. It plays its part, not only in the face of the enemy, but also in personal, organizational and administrative dissonance. Physical courage has the force of urgency of action; moral courage has the weight of responsibility and ethics. The higher the rank, the greater is the relevance of moral courage.

Courage is the most admired of human virtues in all societies and in all walks of life as to be a man is to be courageous. Courage is no less in the higher than in the lower levels of command. Greater the responsibility and higher the rank, the emphasis shifts from physical to moral courage , a much rarer quality, rare but essential to higher leadership.

You need moral courage:

- To say no to an unethical act
- To demand high standards of performance
- To accept one's mistake
- To punish (compassion should not be made an alibi for lack of courage

A courageous leader will do the following:

- Control fear in physical and moral contexts
- Take responsibility for decisions and actions
- Accept responsibility for his own mistakes and shortcomings

- Confront problems directly and take action based on what he believes is right, regardless of what others may think.
- Report on success and failures with equal candor.
- Put him on the line to deal with important problems.
- Support others to make tough decisions.
- Always share mistakes if it will help the team improve.
- Speak up for what he believes is important and then be gracious whether his ideas are accepted or rejected.

Integrity: Do What is Right, Legally and Morally

Leaders of integrity make their principles known and consistently act in accordance with them. The army requires leaders of integrity who possess high moral standards and who are honest in word and deed. Leaders cannot hide what they do. Army leaders say what they mean and do what they say. People of integrity do the right thing not because it is convenient or because they have no choice: but choose the right thing because their character permits them no less.

Integrity is a character trait. It is the willingness to do right, even when we know nobody is watching. It is a moral compass, an inner voice, and it is a basis for trust within a sub-unit, within a unit, within the formation, within any army, worthy of being called the best.

You have integrity if you:

- Always act according to what you know to be right, even at personal cost.
- Possess a high standard of moral values and principles.
- Show good moral judgment and demonstrate

consistent moral behavior.

- Avoid the wrong and stand up for what is right.
- Show candor and fairness in evaluating subordinates' work.
- Use the authority and power that comes with rank to work for mission accomplishment or for soldiers instead of for personal or private gain.
- Put being 'right' ahead of being popular or easy.
- Abide by principles.

Selflessness

It is very much associated with selfless service, i.e. putting the welfare of the nation, the army and subordinate before your own. It is the source of integrity. A selfless person is neither greedy nor looking for shortcuts to success; hence, his integrity never wavers. He seeks no unfair advantage over others; hence honesty comes naturally to him. He is not a self-seeker; hence his loyalty is steady and strong. When a person has such virtues his thoughts, words, and deeds become pure and well integrated. He says what he thinks and does what he says, as such he becomes trustworthy.

Self-Discipline – Be a master of your Habits, not their Slave

Self-discipline is conscious practice of controls, habits and restraints imposed by one and demanded by the profession. These controls and restraints manifest as trained, ingrained responses, in one's conduct and performance of duty. It operates at two levels, personal affairs and personal philosophy. Personal affairs include habits, traits, and practices. They assist in organizing one's life, time, and effort in an orderly fashion and making it readily responsive. Personal philosophy embraces maintenance of human dignity and understanding human psychology on the verge of explosion or excesses.

If you ask me why some people are more successful than others, the simple answer is Self- Discipline. It is the key to personal greatness. It can help you to achieve your goals. Self discipline develops your character. It takes considerable will power to do the right thing in every situation. But the end result is a sense of self-worth and self-esteem. As has been said 'to develop self discipline you must choose to do what you should do when you should do it, whether you feel like it or not".

Importance of Character

This talk of mine would be incomplete if I did not highlight the importance of character. Character, a person's moral and ethical qualities, helps determine what is right and wrong and gives a leader motivation to do what is appropriate, regardless of the consequences. An informed ethical conscience consistent with the army values, which I had mentioned earlier, strengthens leaders to make the right choices when faced with tough issues. Since army leaders seek to do what is right and inspire others to do the same, they must embody these values. Remember, character is essential to successful leadership. It determines who you are and how you act. It helps determine right from wrong and then choose what is right. Becoming a person of character is a career long process involving day-to-day experiences, education, self-development, developmental counseling, coaching, and mentoring. While individuals are responsible for their own character development, you as a leader are responsible for encouraging, supporting and assessing the followers' efforts. Development of character is best done by continual studying, reflection, experience, and feedback.

Conclusion

Gentlemen, it had been my attempt in the past sixty minutes or so to put across some traditionally held views on values as they are building blocks for leadership. Underlying the constants that make our Army what it is, are its values. We must never be complacent about the role of values in our Army. That is why we make a very concerted effort to infuse our values across all ranks of the Army. The Army is a value-based organization that stresses the importance of the team over the individual. Values that emphasize only individual self-interest are cold comfort in times of hardship and danger. Rather, the Army emphasizes 'shared values', the values that make an individual reach beyond self. Army values build strong, cohesive organizations that, in turn, become the source of strength and solidarity for our members in difficult and turbulent times. Value-based leadership means setting the example and then creating a command culture where soldiers can put values into practice. Leaders must not only exemplify army values in their words and deeds, they must create the opportunity for every soldier in their command to live them as well.

Doing right ourselves, teaching what is right to your troops, and encouraging all others with whom you come in contact (including peers and seniors) to do what is right--that is what we are training officers to do, what the services needs them to do and what the nation relies on them to do.

Our experience over the years has taught us that diligence, fairness, sound preparation, professional skill, and loyalty are indeed the hallmarks of our leadership. They are also the best way to give the individual man a solid foundation for living successfully irrespective of his situation. All the time, when the Service seeks to emphasize to its ranks what is the 'right thing to do'; it is speaking of that course of conduct which in the long run is most necessary and useful to the individual. Towards this end, you all must be cognizant of your part in preserving the Army's traditional role as the guarantor of India's fundamental values. And never forget the fact that you as officers, as leaders, must be teachers to show your subordinates how to do what is required and to encourage them to do it.

I am sure that as you progress in your journey in the Army in the years ahead, you as a leader will set the right example for your subordinates to emulate and if this talk of mine is of some help in this direction, I will be more than happy.

PART-III

Miscellaneous Issues Impacting Ethics

9

Ancient Indian Ethos and its Discourse on Ethics*

"India preserves the knowledge that preserves the world."

---Sri Aurobindo

(* Published in 'Door Dhrishti',The Defence Management Journal, Volume IX, Issue 1, July 2014)

Introduction

India, with its rich cultural tradition, has a lot to offer to humanity as a whole on the ways of leading a happy, contended and meaningful life. India is one country where thousands of great souls have been born in every generation and they have shown mankind the way to lead a meaningful life. Hindu spiritual literature is so vast that there is no branch of knowledge that is left un-investigated. Spiritual motive dominates life in India. The *Gita* and the *Upanishads* are often referred to as vehicles of the great systems of thought. The *Puranas* contain the truth couched in myths and stories. It is the intense spirituality of India revealed through its scriptures and epics that has enabled it to resist the ravages of time and the accidents of history.

This essay focuses on the doctrines and ideas from the ancient Indian scriptures and epics. There are two classes of Hindu scriptures- *shruti,* 'that which is heard', and *smriti,* 'tradition' or 'that which is to be remembered'. The *Vedas* and the **Upanishads** fall into the first class of **shruti**. These writings are said to be inspired by God and to have been revealed to humankind by ancient sages called *rishis.* Because of their divine origin, shruti texts are considered to be more sacred than the other class of scriptures, *smriti.* Works that come after the *Vedas* and the *Upanishads* are all *smriti.* These include the *epics, Puranas, Sutras, Shastras,* and the devotional *Bhakti songs.* India boasts of two great *smriti* epics. Both of them, the *Mahabharata* and the *Ramayana,* have had a great influence on Hindu thought. These two great epics have had many layers added to them over the centuries, and both have undergone numerous changes.[1] Besides quotes from these ancient Indian scriptures and epics, this essay also includes some writings of great thinkers, seers and philosophers that India has ever produced including one of India's greatest minds Kautilya, his extraordinary manual on statecraft and the science of living namely the *Arthashastra.* The uniqueness of our country lies in the expression of faith and that it can be expressed with greatest freedom. India has been the home of many realized souls who have illuminated the world.

Indian Ethos

Ethos is a Greek word meaning 'character' that is used to describe the guiding beliefs or ideals that characterize a community, nation, or ideology. It can simply mean the disposition, character, or fundamental values peculiar to a specific person, people, culture, or movement. Ethos forms the root of '*ethikos*' meaning 'moral, showing moral character' which is the origin of the modern English word '*ethics*'. The word '*ethics*' which in Latin is called '*ethicus*' and in Greek called 'ethikos' has come from the word '*ethos*' meaning character or manners. Oxford Dictionary defines ethos as 'the characteristic spirit and beliefs of community/ people' which distinguishes one culture from the other. Indian ethos is drawn from the *Vedas, Upanishads,* the *Bhagavad Gita,* the *Ramayana,* and the *Mahabharata.* Right from the Vedic age it has been discovered that there are two basic universal truths of life, namely, the essential infinitude and divinity of all souls and the essential oneness and solidarity of universe and all life. The expression 'Indian ethos' is an overreaching concept to capture the experiences of Indian civilizations over the centuries. As a result, it is an expansive expression with its beginning in ancient times. Ancient Indian ethos has all the potential to make significant contribution in developing the 'mindset' in leadership and management. Indian ethos has contributed in developing a holistic vision and approach to work ethos. In it is found that all work, be it physical, mental, management, leadership, administration have to be directed towards a single purpose, the manifestation of the essential divinity in man by working for the good of all beings. A spiritual approach to the purpose of life and leadership is presented as an integrated leader's inner perspective such that it forms the foundation for decisions and actions in the outer world in any human endeavor.

While there are several similarities in Indian ethos and western concepts of leadership, the spiritual orientation and non-desire motivated action, distinguish leadership in Indian ethos from that in the western ethos. Indian ethos also indicates that spirituality can serve as foundation for leadership that considers ethics, social responsibility, and concern for environment not just as instruments to protect corporate reputation and income generation, but as fundamental principles and values in their own right. It also reiterates that leaders must be ethical and good corporate citizens. There is no allegiance possible where there is no character in the leader and perfect purity ensures the most lasting allegiance and confidence. The ideal of Indian ethos is best described by the Sanskrit verse: 'ATMANO MOKSHARTHAM JAGAT HITAYA CHA' (For gaining perfection in individual life, as well as, for the welfare of the world)'.

The Message of the Upanishads- The Science of the Self

The *Upanishads* are treasure houses of ancient Hindu philosophy and are among the great seminal books of the world. They have influenced countless generations of men and have given rise to a vast literature in many languages. They are also known as *Vedanta*. The term *Upanishad* literally means, 'sitting down near' or 'sitting close to', and implies listening closely to the mystic doctrines of a spiritual teacher, who has cognized the fundamental truths of the universe. The *Upanishads* form the core of Indian philosophy. They are an amazing collection of writings from original oral transmissions, which have been aptly described by Sri Aurobindo as 'the supreme work of the Indian mind'. The *Upanishads* give us both spiritual vision and philosophical argument, and it is by a strictly personal effort that one can reach the truth. The *Upanishads* gave a permanent orientation to Indian culture by their emphasis on inner penetration and their wholehearted advocacy of what the Greeks later formulated in the dictum 'man, know thyself.' All subsequent developments of Indian culture were powerfully conditioned by this *Upanishad* legacy.[2]

The human being is the central mystery of the universe holding the key to all other mysteries. Indeed, human beings are our own greatest enigma. As the famous physicist Niels Bohr once said, 'We are both spectators and actors in the great drama of existence.' Hence, the importance of developing of what is known as the 'science of human possibilities.' It was such a science that India sought and found in the *Upanishads* in an attempt to unravel the mystery of human beings. Freedom- physical, mental, and spiritual is the watchword of the *Upanishads*. The spiritual insights of the *Upanishads* are an exemption to the tyranny of time. Subsequent scientific advances have not only affected their truth value, but on the contrary, have helped to reveal the rational basis of their insights and enhance their spiritual appeal.[3]

Srimad Bhagavad Gita

Srimad Bhagavad Gita, the divine song cum dialogue of Lord Krishna with his disciple friend, Arjuna, just before the start of Mahabharata war historically dates back to 3102 BC. The dialogue appears in the *Bhishma Parva* of Mahabharata. Bhagavad Gita popularly known as *Gita* contains 18 chapters and 700 stanzas (verses). This dialogue cum song was recorded by author of Mahabharata poet and seer Maharishi Ved Vyasa. *Bhagavad Gita* is the essence and summary of the Vedanta and Vedic philosophy of ancient India. It is the gist of Vedic and Upanishad knowledge of the ancient India, and hence, *Bhagavad Gita* is the most appropriate and authentic representation of ancient Indian ethos. In his book titled *'Timeless Leadership-18 Leadership Sutras from Bhagavad Gita', Shri Debashis* Chatterjee opines 'Krishna literally guides Arjuna through the *ABCs* of leadership. Here, *A represents Authenticity* or truth, which is the core value of leaders; B stands for *Being,* which is the raw material for becoming a leader; and C stands for

Convergence, which a leader achieves between his current reality and his goal, or between a problem and its solution. Indeed as a text, the *Bhagavad Gita* does not separate the problem from the solution. [4]

Just as a tremendous battle is about to begin, Krishna stations Arjuna's chariot between the two armies. Arjuna, overcome with pity and confusion, refuses to fight and asks for Krishna's guidance. There in the battlefield, with arrows flying all around, this rare teaching takes place. Arjuna's purely human predicament on the battlefield of *Kurukshetra* is often viewed by philosophers as a mere fictional setting within which the lofty wisdom of *Gita* is expounded. But in choosing such a setting, Sage Vyasa unequivocally establishes the practical intention of the *Gita.* It is the human predicament which evokes the *Gita,* and it is the predicament of daily life that the *Gita* resolves. There is no significant problem in life which cannot be referred to the *Bhagavad Gita* for a perfect solution. The *Bhagavad Gita* emphasizes not only the spiritual aspects but also the material and psychological import, all interwoven to stress the need for its practical application in all phases of life. Truth is of all-round benefit to man. Because of its character as book of universal wisdom, the *Bhagavad Gita* can be used as the scriptural support for many doctrinal points of view, religious sects, philosophical schools of thought, and even social theory.

The Concept Of 'Dharma' And Its Linkage To Ethics

The word '*Dharma*' is as complex as it is ubiquitous with its usage in bewildering variety of ways within the Indian tradition. The word '*dharma*' (धर्म) in Sanskrit is derived from the root धृ meaning 'to hold', 'to bear', 'to carry' or 'to support'. धारणात् धर्मः-that which holds together or supports is '*Dharma*'. In this sense, *Dharma* encompasses all ethical, moral, social, and other values or principles, code of conduct and behavior which contribute to the well-being, sustenance, and harmonious functioning of individuals, societies and nations and which prevent their disintegration. In a wider sense, it is *Dharma* which sustains and supports the whole world. This word has gathered around itself such richness of meaning and wealth of associations, that it is impossible to translate it into a single word in any other language, Indian or foreign. In many Indian languages the word '*Dharma*' is used to denote 'religion'. However, in Sanskrit, there is no word which is the exact equivalent of 'religion'. The word 'religion' connotes a set of dogmas and beliefs, a code of conduct, a Founder, a Sacred Book and a Church or similar institution. Such a concept of institutionalized religion is alien to Hindu thought. In fact, Hinduism (more properly '*Sanatana Dharma*') accommodates within its fold people with widely differing beliefs and dogmas. It is therefore no wonder that Sanskrit does not have a word which is the exact equivalent of 'religion' in the sense mentioned above. '*Dharma*' is also used in Indian languages to denote 'duty', 'righteousness', 'virtue', 'justice', 'morality', 'charity', 'innate tendency', etc. All these represent only a particular aspect of '*Dharma*'. There is no single word which can be substituted for the Sanskrit word '*Dharma*'. This is also the case with English and other western languages where the difficulty in translating the term is enhanced because of the cultural divide. In fact the word '*Dharma*' has already been assimilated into the lexicon of the English language.

'*Dharma*' is a unique human attribute. The universal law of *Dharma*, though has self-realization as its ultimate goal, does not ignore the life and the way of living in the righteous way, one is expected to reach greater heights in spiritual advancement, at which one might realize the self.[5]

The virtues required for leading a dharmic way of life are available in the form of codes /rules of conduct at many places in the vast spiritual literatures of India. *Manusmriti* or Laws of Manu intimately interrelated in Hindu thought, is an encompassing representation of life in the world--how it is, and how it should be lived. It is about *Dharma* which subsumes the English concepts of 'religion', 'duty', 'right', 'justice', 'practice', and 'principle'. It prescribes the ten rules for the observation of *Dharma* which includes, Patience, Forgiveness, Piety or Self-control, Honesty, Sanctity, Control of senses, Reason, Learning, Truthfulness, and Absence of Anger.[6]

The philosopher Dr.S.Radhakrishnan advancing the 'neo-Hindu' agenda maintained that *Dharma* 'is the norm which sustains the universe, the principle of a thing by virtue of which it is vital to what it is'. And a 'person who follows the *Dharma* realizes the ideal of his own character and maintains the eternal lawfulness in himself'. Thus, the basic principle of *Dharma* is the realization of the dignity of the human spirit.[7]

Trigunas –A Vedic Interpretation

> *"In the state of Sattva, a man is neither satisfied by fulfilling his physical desires not consented to remain within the limits of his intellect, but stands steadily keeping the balance between both. In this state alone he can discriminate properly. Sattva gives equilibrium and enables us to think and act rightly."*
>
> **-Swami Paramananda**

The age old Indian scriptures have in them the highest wisdom on human characteristics and human behavior. In Hinduism, the concept of `Gunas' plays an important role as they are more than just psychological states. In Sanskrit, the word Guna means, 'That which binds'. Guna is also translated as 'way of being' defined by three Vedic factors namely 'Sattva, Rajas and Tamas'. The attributes of the three basic Vedic factors of personality, i.e. Gunas are as follows[8]:

- Sattva is synonymous with purity, intelligence and is experienced as perception of wisdom, lightness of being, and zest for acquiring knowledge. Individuals in which this Guna dominates are, natural academics, healers, spiritual leaders, etc. The flip side of Sattva is the attachment to knowledge, happiness, incapacity to bear physical pain, lack of initiative, etc.
- Rajas are synonymous with energy and action and are experienced as ambition, zest for acquiring material benefits, rigorous activity, will-power, ability to bear pain, and competition. Individuals in whom this Guna dominates are, natural leaders, politicians, captains of industry, military, etc. The flip side of Rajas is anger, passion, attachment to activity, and possessions.
- Tamas is synonymous with materiality, density, dullness, and inertia and is experienced as a state of rest/sleep, mental inactivity/lethargy, insensitivity/irresponsibility and inertia. Individuals in which this Guna dominates are natural for simple, well-defined, repetitive tasks which are performed by the labour force, artisans etc. The flip side of this Guna are laziness, cheating tendency, greed, frustration, and in extreme cases aggression, vindictiveness, addiction, perversion, and self-destruction. It may be hard to believe as to how such extremely subtle Gunas could have taken the form of this gross and tangible world. Though it is a difficult proposition to imagine, science has of late come out with findings in support of this concept. Though all Gunas are present in an individual, only one of the three Gunas dominates and the individual behaves according to the Guna that is dominant. Our nature contains, apart from its passionate 'rajasic' and its downward-tending

'tamasic' quality, a purer 'satwic' element and it is the encouragement of this, the highest part, which is the business of ethics.

Purusharthas - Aims of Life

The idea of *Purusharthas* has played a very vital role in the history of Indian thought. The term '*Purusharthas*', literally signifies 'what is sought by men' so that it may be taken as equivalent to a human end or purpose. We know that a man, like other living beings, act instinctively; but he can also do so deliberately. This means he can consciously set before himself ends, and work for them. It is this conscious pursuit that transforms them into *Purusharthas*. Thus, even the ends which man shares with other animal, like food and rest, may become *Purusharthas* provided they are sought knowingly. We may, thus, define a *Purushartha* as an end which is consciously sought to be accomplished either for its own sake or for the sake of utilizing it as a means to the accomplishment of further end or goal.

The Purusharthas that have been recognized in India from very early times are four: *Dharma (duty), Artha (wealth), Kama (pleasure), and Moksha (liberation)*. Of the four, *Dharma* and *Moksha* are the one that man ought to seek but ordinarily does not; while *Artha* and *Kama* are the one that man is naturally inclined to seek. Human life without purpose would be meaningless. One needs to have an end or purpose in life towards which our actions can be directed. *Dharma, Artha, Kama, and Moksha* are the aims or goals of human life which man ought to strive for attaining it throughout his life, and in all births. These '*arthas*' are meant for the '*purusha*' meaning 'meant for the human being'. Till man lives or the species of human beings is alive, *purusharthas* are going to add meaning to our life. It was there earlier; it is sought today, and is going to be there till man lives.[9]

Of the four objectives stated above, *Dharma* has always occupied the premier place. It not only signifies an absolute and immutable concept of righteousness but also includes the idea of duty which every human being owes to himself. *Dharma* is law in its widest sense--spiritual, moral, ethical, and temporal. When society respected *Dharma*, society protected itself; when society offended it, society undermined itself.

Theory of "Nishkama Karma"

"The wise, possessed with knowledge, renouncing the fruits of their actions, becomes freed from the bondage of birth and death and reach that state which is beyond all evil."

-Chapter 2, Verse 51, The Bhagavad Gita.

The word '*Karma*' denotes action. It denotes actions that bring back results. The theory of *Karma* is to the spiritual world, just like the law of cause and effect. Every physical act of a person is a deed. His/her speech and words are deeds. Even his/her thoughts are deeds. Every word or action generates an appropriate reaction and is weighed on the scales of eternal justice. As per Hinduism, nobody can get away from the clutches of *Karma*.

To understand the attributes of '*Nishkama Karma*', we need to understand it's opposite, namely, the '*Sakam Karma*' which is the action performed in expectation of something. Expectations never end. When one expectation is fulfilled, another arises and there is no end to the expectations. Hence, those who perform '*Sakam Karma*', simply waste their efforts irrespective of whether they perform good or bad karma. On the contrary, no effort is wasted in the path of '*Nishkama karma*'. Every small effort is satisfying. There is always fulfillment. The formula for `*Nishkama karma*' is '*Karma minus Kamana*' (desire).

As per Hinduism, freedom from the cycle of birth and

death is the ultimate objective and it can be achieved by adherence to the doctrine of '*Nishkama Karma*'. According to this doctrine, an individual who performs actions without attachment to the fruits is freed from the bondage of birth and death, thereby, attaining a state beyond all suffering. The theme of *Nishkama Karma* is best described by this verse from *Gita*:

> *"Karmanye Vadhikaraste, Ma Phaleshou Kada Chana! Ma Karma Phala Hetur Bhurmatey Sangostva Akarmani"*
>
> **—Srimad Bhagavad Gita, Chapter 2, Verse 47.**
>
> *It means: To action alone hast though a right and never at all to its fruits; let not the fruits of action be thy motive; neither let here be in thee any attachment to inaction.*

The Ethics of Manu Dharma Sastra (Manu Smriti)

This ancient Hindu law book marks an important phase in the development of ethical thought in India. The fundamental objective of any law book is to establish a legal system. Manu Smriti considers in addition to legal maxims, certain religious, political, moral, economic, and metaphysical principles providing consistent justification for its social theory. Manu Smriti adopts certain philosophical views of different schools of thought to project a systematic ethical theory to back its legal system. In terms of authority and reverence, it occupies an important place next only to the Vedas from which it derives its authority. It enumerates the scriptures, the tradition, the conduct of virtuous men, and self-satisfaction as the four major sources of the sacred law and morality.

Manu classifies *Dharma* or one's ethical obligations into twofold: `*Sadharana Dharma*' and `*Visista Dharma*'. While the former refers to the common duties of higher three castes, the latter refers to the duties relative to one's castes and particular stage in life. Manu enumerates steadfastedness (Dhairya), forgiveness (Kshama), application (Dharma), non-appropriation (Chowryabhava), cleanliness (Swachcha). repression of senses (Indriyanigraha), wisdom (Dhi), learning (Vidhya), veracity (Satya), and restraint from anger (Akrodha) as the ten-fold virtues intended for individual perfection.[10] Both these Dharma's as stated above,form Manu's moral prescription.

Ethical Debates in Indian Epics

Ramayana and Mahabharata are the two epics which have so mingled with the collective conscience of our people that, to this day, the ideas and values in them continue to influence our lives. In fact no discussion of Indian ethos or serious study of Indian culture can avoid an interpretation of these epics. It is almost a truism, whether we realize it or not, that we in India, still live under the spell of these epics. Examples are often cited as rationale for our social actions which are often based on contrary interpretations of the same event.

Both the 'Utilitarianism' and 'Kantianism' ethical theories can be found in these epics. As opposed to Lord Rama's 'dharma' in Ramayana, Lord Krishna's point of view was flexible. The 'means' and 'ends' analysis is significant. From one perspective it appears that for Lord Rama, piousness of both means and ends are significant and for Lord Krishna, only end matters. Whereas from other perspective both of them seem to hold 'deontological' point of view.[11] Deontology provides insight into the moral character of individual acts.

A significant portion of both the renowned Indian epic '*The Ramayana*' and '*The Mahabharata*' deal with moral dilemmas. These moral dilemmas are universal in the sense that they mostly represent a conflict in the state of mind and are found in everyday life. Various methods of resolution or dissolution of moral dilemmas can be delineated in these epics. A classic example of this dilemma comes from the *Bhagavad Gita* where *Arjuna* is faced with an awesome dilemma. In the battlefield into which his chariot is driven, he is confronted by his close relatives and kinsmen whose treachery and unconscionable behavior has brought about the war he has to engage in. If justice has to prevail, he must fight and kill them. *Arjuna* breaks down and wants to lay down his arms but *Lord Krishna,* who is acting as his charioteer, convinces him that he has to do his duty as a warrior. The idea of duty is what mediates between having an imperative and the performance of the course of action demanded. One has to transcend moral distinctions to do one's duties with an inner freedom to work with an enlightened intelligence to act. The Hindu concept of '*Dharma*' is a constant elaboration of this point. The '*Sanatana Dharma' (the Eternal Religion)* derives its authority from its truth-character and not from any person, be he a saint or even an incarnation; and the truth-character of a teaching demands, it be verifiable by all irrespective of dogma, creed, and race and at all times. [12]

Kautilya's Arthashastra

Kautilya also known as Chanakya and Vishnugupta, wrote the *Arthashastra* in the second century AD. It is the oldest and most exhaustive treatise on statecraft and on issues of diplomacy, war, peace, intelligence, and political economy. It stands out in the corpus of the rich but under-explored ancient history of India. '*Artha*' literally meaning 'wealth' is one of the four supreme aims of life prescribed by ancient Indian (Hindu) philosophy the other three aims being *Dharma (Righteousness), Kama (Desires)* and *Moksha (Liberation). Arthashastra* has much wider significance and the material prosperity of individual is just a part of it. It is an ancient Indian treatise on statecraft, economic policy and military strategy. It is an extraordinary manual and a pioneering work in public administration. The commentaries on Kautilya's *Arthashastra* highlight its political, diplomatic, and administrative insights. For ages, rulers of the world over have referred to Kautilya's *Arthashastra* for building a nation on sound economics and spiritual values. It has been rightly referred to as 'knowledge of wealth and a wealth of knowledge'. Kautilya's greatest contribution was to conceptualize the state as a set of functions. These functions required not merely a definition of the government but a much fuller explanation of what constituted the state. *Arthashastra* views the man in leadership position as '*Vijigsu*', i.e. desirous of victory. It is an all encompassing phrase denoting overall achievement orientation guided by the principle of '*Yogakshema*' implying well-being, happiness, prosperity and security of the subjects or the organizational members. *Arthashastra* deals, in detail, with the qualities and disciplines required for a '*Rajarishi*', wise and virtuous, prudent, and ethical king/leader. Kautilya's prescriptions for control of senses are wisdom fit for a manual of leadership and command for the military, as well as for all leadership roles in the society.

On the use of authority or power to punish (*danda*), Kautilya cautions his 'ideal king' to use it judiciously and to protect the weak from the stronger. Thus, a leader is advised not to misuse his power or authority. He indicates that an unjust or improper use of authority may lead to serious consequences. A leader who has no self-control and gives himself up to excessive indulgences in pleasures will soon perish (Book 1, Chapter 6, and Sutra 4).

Sri Aurobindo on Ethics

Sri Aurobindo (15 Aug 1872-5th Dec 1950) is undoubtedly the greatest thinker, philosopher, seer, and yogi that India has ever produced. He has left behind for posterity his extensive writings on a variety of subjects. He opines that 'True ethics is Dharma', the right fulfillment and working of the higher nature, and right action should have the right motive. Right action should be its own justification and not go limping on the crutches of greed and fear. Right done for its own sake is truly ethical and ennobles the growing spirit. Right done in the lust for a material reward or from fear of avenging stripes of the executioner or sentence of the judge, may be eminently practical, but is a lowering of the soul of man; or at least the principle is a concession to his baser animal and unspiritual nature'.[13]

Sri Aurobindo in his writings on Gita seeks to fix the principle of action deeper in the centre of man's soul and points us ultimately to the government of outward life by the divine self within.[14] Sri Aurobindo in his writings on Ethics had maintained that reason alone does not lead us to addressing ethical dilemmas we all face and we need to look at things not only from the rational point of view but add to it a deeper psychological and spiritual view. Reason can never give the true ethical solution; solution lies above the reason. He goes on to state that 'There is only one safe rule for the ethical man, to stick to his principle of good, his instinct for good, his vision of good, his intuition of good and to govern by that his conduct. He may err, but he will be on his right road in spite of all stumblings, because he will be faithful to the law of his nature.' The saying of the Gita is always true; *better is the law of one's own nature though ill-performed, dangerous is an alien law however speciously superior it may seem to our reason.* But the law of nature of the ethical being is the pursuit of good; it can never be the pursuit of utility.

Swami Vivekananda on 'Morality and Ethics'

Swami Vivekananda, an Indian Hindu monk and chief

disciple of the 19th century saint Ramakrishna was a key figure in the introduction of the Indian philosophies of Vedanta and Yoga to the Western world. He is credited with raising inter-faith awareness, bringing Hinduism to the status of a major world religion during the late 19th century. He was a major force in the revival of Hinduism in India, and contributed to the concept of nationalism in colonial India. Vivekananda founded the Ramakrishna Math and the Ramakrishna Mission. He is perhaps best known for his inspiring speech which began, "Sisters and Brothers of America ...," in which he introduced Hinduism at the Parliament of the World's Religions in Chicago in 1893. Vivekananda conducted hundreds of public and private lectures and classes, disseminating tenets of Hindu philosophy in the United States, England, and Europe. In India, Vivekananda is regarded as a patriotic saint and his birthday is celebrated as National Youth Day in India.[15]

As per Swami Vivekananda, 'The prevalent morality, in both individual life and social life , is mostly based on fear -fear of the police, fear of the public ridicule, fear of God's punishment, fear of Karma , and so on' The current theory of ethics also does not explain why a person should be moral and be good to others. Principle of morality should be based on intrinsic purity and oneness of 'Atman'. We should be pure because purity is our real nature, our true Divine self or Atman. Similarly, we should love and serve our neighbors because we are all one in the supreme spirit known as Paramatman or Brahman.[16] A well known quote attributed to Swami Vivekananda reads "all the secrets of success are there to pay as much attention to the means as to the end. Ethics itself is not the end but the means to the end".

Thirukkural-A Text Book on Moral Life

'Thirukkural', is a classic of couplets or Kurals (1330 rhyming Tamil couplets) or aphorisms. It was authored by

Thiruvalluvar, a poet who is said to have lived anytime between 2nd century BCE and 5th century CE. Most believe he wrote Thirukkural in 30 BC which is part of Tamil Sangam period. Though it cannot be called a scripture or an epic, it is ranked as an extra-ordinary treatise on the 'Art of Living.' It dwells deep into the unshifting foundations of human life and attempts to provide guidance, not only for the society in general but for each individual whatever be his /her vocation or profession. In Part -1 of the compilation on 'Virtue', there is a very apt reference to 'Truthfulness' (verses 291-300), one of the most desirable virtues in the path of righteousness.

"All the world esteems a truthful man, for whom
Other virtues come without any effort" (Verse 296)

Such a man does not have to undergo privations and penance to merit other virtues. These virtues come automatically to a man of truth.

Spirituality and Ethics

There is little agreement between scholars, practitioners, and social commentators as to what is meant by spirituality, nor is there consensus on how it might be related to religion. Some opine that in practical terms religion and spirituality are overlapping concepts which cannot be separated and contrasted in a clear-cut manner. A popular and inclusive rather than an exclusive definition of spirituality is stated : 'Spirituality is the personal quest for understanding answers to ultimate questions about life, about meaning, and about relationships to the sacred or transcendent'.[17]

Dr S. Radhakrishnan in his book titled 'Indian Philosophy' has remarked that 'Indian philosophy is essentially spiritual' and which illustrates the 'endless quest of the mind, ever old, ever new'. Next to the category of reality, the concept of '*Dharma*' occupies a prime spot and he goes on to highlight that 'ethical perfection is the first step towards divine knowledge'.[18] He has shown that in their perception of the goal, in the acuteness of their reasoning, and in the boldness of their conception, the Indian thinkers are second to none.

As a bird needs two wings to fly, so a human being needs two wings of existence: the spiritual and the material, to lead a natural and harmonious life. Spirituality teaches us to balance our aspirations in these two fields. However, in today's world the demands of material living call out so loudly that they often capture the lion's share of our attention. By contrast, the call of spirituality sometimes referred to as 'the still, and small voice within' is subtle and quiet. Considering the demands of daily living that compete for our attention, it takes a special determination to make room for our inner life. As we invest ourselves in our spiritual growth our understanding develops, our capacity for growth expands and we experience greater energy and enthusiasm for ethical living. We begin to look forward to our spiritual practice and to anticipate its nourishing benefit. Eventually, it becomes a natural and indispensable part of our existence. The whole idea of Spirituality is to revive in us, the true inner being-the Self. Spirituality is the need for an inner existence.[19]

Morality is the ordinary view that a well-regulated individual and social conduct keeps society going and lead towards a better, a more rational, temperate, sympathetic, self-restrained dealing with our fellow human beings. But ethics in the spiritual point of view is much more. It is a means of developing in our actions and still more essentially in the character of our being the diviner self in us, a step of growing into the nature of the Godhead.[20] Indian spiritual writings lay stress upon not so much the quality of the action to be done but the quality of the soul from which the action flows, upon its truth, fearlessness, purity, love, compassion, benevolence, and upon the actions as their outflowings.This can be done best by realizing God as the higher Self, the guiding and uplifting will or the master whom we love and serve. Not fear of Him, but love of Him and aspiration to the freedom and eternal purity of His being must be the motive.[21]

Conclusion

India is a secular state and it derives its values from many of her religious scriptures and teachings. *Bhagavad Gita (song of God),* a revered Hindu religious text of about 700 verses, written well over two thousand years ago, contains an immense wealth of ageless wisdom, weaving together in its eighteen chapters, a battlefield conversation, a narrative on the problems faced by leaders from a perspective that is both compelling and contemporary. In the '*Upanishads*', we get an intelligible body of verified and verifiable spiritual insights leading man irrespective of creed or race, to his realization in his own life. The law book of '*Yajnavalkya*' (a famous philosopher and a sage who finds a mention in Mahabharata), states where there is conflict between righteousness and material advantage (*Dharma and Artha*), the former should prevail. '*Dharma*' is the central ethical concept and a very comprehensive ethical category in the light of which all the ethical ideals can be understood. *Dharma*, the moral pursuit of man is to be followed in all the human endeavors and it underlies all the other '*Purusharthas*' namely '*Artha*' (wealth) 'Kama' (desired pleasures), and '*Moksha*' (spiritual liberation)

Right from Rig Vedic times to the present day environments, the evolution of Indian ethical values has been a continuous process, which forms a grand uniform edition despite many invasions of other cultures and faiths. There are certain fundamental notions which run throughout the history of our country. These foundations are not merely part of intellectual or ethical speculations but form the nucleus of a living tradition. The popular morality and ethical beliefs have their sources in ancient humanistic ethos.[22] In his seminal work, Gurcharan Das in his book 'The Difficulty of Being Good-On the Subtle Art of Dharma' draws our attention as how extraordinary a word and idea '*Dharma*' has evolved from the ancient Rig Veda and enriched itself over three thousand years through a process of contestation and adaptation.[23] What emerges is a doctrine that we can apply to life itself. The greater practical part of the *Dharma* is ethical; it is the idea of the moral law.[24] Rights and duties are harmonized in the lofty ideal of *Dharma*, whose discovery is contingent upon the prior discovery of the *Dharma* of a leader, of a citizen, a worker, a teacher, a student, a doctor, an engineer, a clerk, a manager, an officer, a soldier, an industrialist, a cleaner, an artist, an artisan, a mother, a woman, a man: everyone who is an Indian. This idea of India representing the Indian ethos, therefore, first asks each one of us to discover ourselves.

"But when you move amidst the world free from attachment and aversion alike, there comes the peace in which all sorrows end; and you are in the wisdom of the Self."

--Bhagavad Gita 2:64-65.

This essay has been a modest attempt by the author to give a very broad overview of the discourse on ethics as gleaned from our scriptures and epics, a short outline of a vast subject. It has no pretensions to completeness in any sense of the term. It is aimed to awaken, if possible in some measure, the interest for it to which it is so justly entitled. India and her ethos is so varied that it has something to appeal to everyone, no matter what level of development and field of activity the person is engaged in. It is like a beacon guiding the souls in search and hungry for true spirituality. That is the variety that Mother India has to offer as a high place of refuge for the multitudes after great upheavals.

India is characterized by a diversity of religious beliefs and practices. Apart from the most dominant religion i.e. Hinduism, other religions practiced in India - Christianity, Islam, Sikhism, Jainism, Buddhism and others—their influence on human behavior has been indeed very noteworthy. Throughout India's history, her ethos has been influenced by the religious demographics of the country. And in the inevitable conflict of values, very often, religion and philosophy offer very strikingly different perceptions. Our vision would have been very greatly impaired without the insights offered by such religions and faiths and their enlightened interpreters.

References

1. 'About Hindu Scriptures-Myads.org at myads. org/nirmal/hinduism/script.html.
2. Subhamoy Das –'The Upanishads (Vedanta)-What are Upanishads?' at www.hinduism.about.com.
3. 'What the Upanishads contain' by Swami Ranganathananda in "Message of the Upanishads", pp 4-5.
4. Debashis Chatterjee in "Timeless Leadership-18 Leadership Sutras from Sri Bhagavad Gita, p xvii.
5. "Gleanings from Sanskrit Literature: DHARMA-Its wider meaning and Connotations available at 'prramurthy1931.blogspot.in.'
6. K. Nagarajan –"*Indian Ethos and Values for Leadership Excellence*"; Chapter 10-'Dharma and its Relevance to Leaders', p118, New Age International Publishers, First Edition, 2011.

7. S. Radhakrishnan, *'Religion and Society'*, London:George Allen and Unwin, 1952, pp107-08.
8. 'Development of equivalent Indian metrics of Personality types'-A thesis submitted for the award of Master of philosophy in management by Gp Capt C.R. Mohan, VSM.
9. Ms. Sneha Sharma- "Purusharthas-Aims of Life" available at Joshi - *Bedekar College, Thane/ website* : www.vpmthane.org.
10. Illa Ravi –*'Foundations of Indian Ethics -Ethics of Manu Dharma Sastra'*, Kaveri Books, New Delhi, pp 89-141.
11. Dr K.C. Pandey in *"Ethics and Epics--Reflection on Indian Ethos"*, p 3, 'Read Worthy' New Delhi Publications.
12 Swami Ranganathananda in "*The Message of the* Upanishads", p 10.
13. Sri Aurobindo Birth Centenary Library, Volume 16, p 164.
14. *ibid*, Volume 17, p266.
15. Vivekananda at en.wikipedia.org/wiki/Vivekananda
16. Swami Vivekananda: Life and Teachings-Belur Math at www.belurmath.org/swamivivekkanada.
17. Amanda Giles-"Spiritual Intelligence: is it relevant to ethical leadership education at the strategic level of UK defence?"-Defence Academy of the United Kingdom,p8(quoting Koenig et al, 2001, p 18)
18. Dr S Radhakrishnan –*"Indian Philosophy"* Volume 1, pp 21-60.
19. "What is Spirituality?"-Sahaj Marg-System of Raja Yoga Meditation available at www.sahajmarg.org.
20. Sri Aurobindo Birth Centenary Library, Volume 14, p 429.

21 ibid , Volume 21,pp.540-541.

22. *Foundations of Indian Ethos* –Illa Ravi, Kaveri Books, New Delhi, pp 252-269.

23. Gurcharan Das-'*The Difficulty of Being Good-The Subtle Art of Dharma*',p 311.

24. Sri Aurobindo Centenary Library Volume 15, pp 138-142.

10

Ethics for Executives: The Executive as Moral Individual*

"It is not enough to espouse high standards. To live up to them and help others to do the same-requires an ethical cast of mind that lets you practice your principles consistently."

Howard Gardner 'The Ethical Mind'

(*Talk addressed to Senior and Mid-level Executives of *M/S ASTER(Private Limited)*—a professionally driven infra-engineering company providing a wide range of products and services to address customer requirements, primarily in the power and telecom infrastructure segments.)

Preamble

At the outset I would like to thank Brig (retired) JP Singh, CEO, ASTER (Hyderabad Division) for his kind introductory remarks. Few weeks back, he called me up and asked, if I could give a talk to you, all senior and mid-level executives of M/s ASTER Private Limited on 'Ethics'. He also mentioned that apart from many other responsibilities he shoulders, he is also the 'Ombudsman' of the Company. As a conscience keeper, an organizational ombudsman has many roles to play. Among many important portfolios he would be handling, he is also the man for offering coaching on ethical issues. It is probably this concern of his that has prompted him to ask me to give a talk on 'Ethics for Executives'.

You are all aware of the much talked about price fixing and conflicts of interests in business and government including the Security forces. The ethics of many top-level executives have been questioned; the reputations of many organizations have suffered. Much of the argument, it seems to me, is confused. The controversy does not seem to be getting us anywhere. Unfortunately, 'business ethics' is one of those phrases used by all with a different meaning for each user, and indeed, a different meaning at different times when used by the same person. 'Business' means so many things to so many people that when used as an adjective to modify the noun 'ethics' which itself is a term meaning many things to many people, the resultant phrase becomes confusing.

Undoubtedly ethical conduct has always been a problem of some proportion, but in today's competitive business environment, perhaps it is even more so. Illegal and unethical behavior persists even as efforts to expose it often succeed in making its rewards short lived. It is against such a backdrop, that I decided to share some thoughts with all of you on ***'Ethics for Executives-The Executive as Moral Individual'.***

Introduction

When you ask someone to speak about ethics, I reckon it invariably ends up as a 'sermon' from some high pedestal. This sermon often takes the form of 'Commandments/ Maxims' tersely worded as 'Thou Shall Not'. They are external in character and prohibitive in kind, and by their very phrasing, create an attitude of suspicion on the part of the public. As I was setting about preparing my lecture script, I was wondering if ethics without a sermon is feasible/practical/convincing. Can I attempt to convert these 'Thou shall not' diktats with 'Yes you can' positive assertions? I have tried my best, but this morning as I was going through my script, I noticed I had also fallen into this trap knowingly or unknowingly. I reckon on a subject like ethics this is perhaps unavoidable.

Many questions also came to my mind:

- How ethical are Businessmen? Do they have an internally developed code of conduct that can be and is professed as the code by which members of the profession live?
- What makes a business executive successful? Is it the size of profit, his sense of personal fulfillment, the approval of others, or is he seeking a greater meaning of his business in the context of his business experience?
- Do you tell your boss you have flu when you just need a day to relax? Or keep that extra money the bank teller mistakenly hands you or tell little white lies for simple convenience?
- Are you almost ethical, but not quite? And when is the harm done?
- Is there a confusion and controversy about

'Corporate morality' and 'Business ethics'? If so how does it get resolved?

- Is good business also good ethics?
- Is following strict ethical code good for a business in the long run?

Here I am reminded of the Five Ts, *Truth, Trust, Tolerance, Transparency* and *Tact,* which stands out as cardinal reference points in the ethical arena. Take the example of Satyam Computer Services Limited. The word 'Satyam' means Truth, and look what happened when truth was forsaken. "TRUST", Global Trust Bank. Trust was the middle name of the company. What happened when trust was belied? Likewise, you have many instances where values of tolerance, transparency, and tact are not lived out contributing to the present crisis of leadership.

Core Definition of Ethics and Values

I would like to pause for a while and reflect on the 'Core definition of ethics and values.' I reckon, it may be little presumptuous on my part to discuss this amongst this well informed audience, but it is good to have our basics clear, for you will agree that many ethical patterns are in vogue, wherein, many strands of ethical traditions have been woven together. We have such a diverse inheritance of ethical ways that no matter which one we choose, the others are, at least, to some degree betrayed. The word 'ethics' owes its origin to the great Greek philosophers, Plato, Socrates, and Aristotle and it is a literal translation of the word 'ethos' which means habitual or customary conduct. To Aristotle, ethics meant the study of excellence in the virtues of character. Closer home, the '*Bhagavad Gita*' propounded the concept of '*Dharma*' or '*righteousness*' or doing one's duty when engaged in any vocation or profession.

Ethics is concerned with the kinds of values and morals an individual or a society finds desirable or appropriate. Furthermore, ethics is concerned with the virtuousness of individuals and their motives. Ethical theory provides a system of rules or principles that guide us in making decisions about what is right or wrong and good or bad in a particular situation. It provides a basis for understanding what is it to be a morally decent human being. For those of you, in the senior management positions, in your leadership role, ethics has to do with what leaders do and who leaders are. It is deals with the nature of leaders' behavior, and with their virtuousness. In any decision making situation, ethical issues are either implicitly or explicitly involved. The choices leaders make and how they respond in a given circumstance are informed and directed by their ethics. Decisions large and small, policies guided or instinctive, one after another finally establish what the corporation's ethical level is to be.

Few years ago, sociologist Raymond Baumhart asked business people, "What do ethics mean to you?" Among their replies were the following:

"Ethics has to do with what my feelings tell me is right or wrong."
"Ethics has to do with my religious beliefs."
"Being ethical is doing what the law requires."
"Ethics consists of the standards of behavior our society accepts."
"I don't know what the word means."

These replies might be typical of our own. The meaning of 'ethics' is hard to pin down, and the views many people have about ethics are shaky. Like Baumhart's first respondent, many people tend to equate ethics with their feelings. But being ethical is clearly not a matter of following one's feelings. A person following his or her feelings may recoil from doing what is right. In fact, feelings frequently deviate from what is ethical.

Nor should one identify ethics with religion. Most

religions, of course, advocate high ethical standards. Yet if ethics were confined to religion, then ethics would apply only to religious people. But ethics applies as much to the behavior of the atheist as to that of the saint. Religion can set high ethical standards and can provide intense motivations for ethical behavior. Ethics, however, cannot be confined to religion nor is it the same as religion.

Being ethical is also not the same as following the law. The law often incorporates ethical standards to which most citizens subscribe. But laws, like feelings, can deviate from what is ethical. American pre-Civil War slavery laws and the apartheid laws of yesteryears in South Africa are grotesquely obvious examples of laws that deviate from what is ethical.

Finally, being ethical is not the same as doing 'whatever society accepts.' In any society, most people accept standards that are, in fact, ethical. But standards of behavior in society can deviate from what is ethical. An entire society can become ethically corrupt. Nazi Germany is a good example of a morally corrupt society. If being ethical were doing 'whatever society accepts,' then to find out what is ethical one would have to find out what society accepts. To decide what I should think about abortion, for example, I would have to take a survey of our society and then conform my beliefs to whatever society accepts. But no one ever tries to decide an ethical issue by doing a survey. The lack of social consensus on many issues makes it impossible to equate ethics with whatever society accepts. Some people accept abortion, but many others do not. If being ethical were doing whatever society accepts, one would have to find an agreement on issues which does not, in fact, exist.

What, then, is ethics? In contemporary times, ethics is two things. Firstly, ethics refers to well based standards of right and wrong that prescribe what humans ought to do, usually in terms of rights, obligations, benefits to society, fairness, or specific virtues. Secondly, ethics refers to the study and development of one's ethical standards. It is necessary to constantly examine one's standards to ensure that they are reasonable and well-founded. Ethics also means, then, the continuous effort of studying our own moral beliefs and our moral conduct, and striving to ensure that we and the institutions we help to shape, live up to standards that are reasonable and solidly-based. It is incumbent on all of us to take a hard look at ourselves to see if our ethical behavior is what it should be. This is of particular concern to you all, as you represent a chosen set of executives to listen to this talk based on your managerial credentials and, as you move along the path of career advancement, you should ensure frequent azimuth checks with your ethical compass. We must master ethical distinctions to enable clear ethical thinking. We must commit in advance to ethical principles so that we can exercise disciplined decision making skills to choose wisely.

Values

In fact no discussion on ethics would be complete without highlighting the relevance and importance of values. True leadership cannot be said to exist if it is not value based and ethical in character. Exceptional performance comes only under exceptional leadership and commitment to sets of values and forms of conduct. Concise Oxford Dictionary defines values as one's principles or standards; one's judgment of what is important in life. What emerges clearly is the fact that values are personal bench marks that are greatly influenced by parents, teachers, mentors, peers, and superiors. The environment more than anything else, has also become the scapegoat for decaying values.

How do values relate to ethics? One of the keys is in the phrase: 'Values are what we, as a profession, judge to be right.' Individually or organizationally, values determine what is right and what is wrong, and doing what is right or wrong is what we mean by ethics. To behave ethically is to behave in a manner consistent with what is right or moral. What does 'generally considered to be right' mean? That is a critical question, and part of the difficulty in deciding whether or not behavior is ethical is in determining what is right or wrong.

Erosion of Values

There is a broad agreement among thinking people in our country that our values have deteriorated over the decades, if not actually been lost. Corruption in all its dimensions, graft, crime, unwillingness to insist on the right values even when they are known and individually respected, are now by-words in our society. It is well recognized that moral values and ethics are imbibed by people from the environment in which they grow up, the teaching they receive from the education (formal and informal) process they go through, religion and its interpretations, the example of others, especially those who become their role models, etc.

Personal convictions –same as a critical driver in value-based character develop from family, community, education, religious/spiritual upbringing, and peer influence. These convictions form the bedrock of moral character, shaping it long before the individual joins any profession. But rapid and extensive changes in the lives of people have been leading to trends that need to be acknowledged. You will have a large number of your work force affected by some of the influences as mentioned below:

- **Socio-Economic Milieu**—India is going through phenomenal transitions in socio-economic terms which are altering the main structures that create the basis of moral values and their practice. While we see the traditional foundations are weakening, the new ones have yet to emerge. The point of concern is that we do not seem to be making sufficient effort to conceptualize and internalize the traditional values required in the new socio-economic milieu.

- **Increasing consumerism**—Rapidly rising expectations and increasing gap between aspirations and realities have triggered a rising sense of relative deprivation, with a strong urge to improve one's own quality of life as quickly as possible, jettisoning moral values and concerns about the common good. There is a growing degree of cynicism in society.
- **Breakdown of the Joint family system**—The family structure and its influence are increasingly under stress. In particular the joint family systems are dissolving into nuclear families where working parents are able to devote much less time to inculcating moral and ethical values in children.
- **Education system**—School education has been losing its moral punch since it now places heavy emphasis on academic studies and a very high percentage of marks are needed for college admissions, with the result that very little attention is given to all round character development.
- **Peer influence**—It has been leaning towards greater personal freedom and lower emphasis on doing the right thing under the rubric of 'realism'; the general thinking in society today is that 'if it does not hurt anyone else, then I can do whatever I wish' or 'What I do in my private life is my business'.
- **Rapidly increasing urbanization**—Rising prosperity and concurrent in-equities and a host of other factors that have increased the potential for occurrence of turbulence in society. Morals and ethics get

buffeted by such turbulence at an early stage itself, leaving many individuals confused and even ignorant of what is critical beyond the glitter of modern consumerist life.

- **Influence of Religion**—While religion has assumed greater salience as an emotional anchor, its ritualization and exploitation for narrow (mostly material) ends has deprived society of the opportunity to use it for strengthening moral values.

Hardly a day goes by when we are not tempted to compromise. In the real world, busy schedules, and conflicts of interests cause us to act in ways that clash with our beliefs. Ethical compromise, big or small, dulls our sense of where to draw the line. It instills a habit of distorted thinking and puts us at risk of losing control of our decisions. This brings me to the point regarding 'Ethical Dilemmas'.

Ethical Dilemmas

An ethical dilemma, by its very nature, places the moral decision maker in a situation with competing virtues or values; in a true ethical dilemma, two or more of the possible solutions have merit and ethical support. If an actor is placed in a situation where there is only one ethical answer, it is not a dilemma- it is a case of having the moral courage to do what is obvious. The fact is that the values themselves can sometimes come into conflict with each other – a situation that is the basis of ethical dilemmas. Such dilemmas never involve a choice between 'right' versus 'wrong,' but rather a choice between two apparent 'rights.' Hence, dilemmas essentially consist of competing values that we consider important, but which we cannot simultaneously honor.

To bring clarity to an ethical dilemma, it is useful to define the problem – the ethical dilemma – in terms of a 'right versus right' conflict. There are four common 'right versus right' dilemmas that can be used to define the problem – truth versus loyalty, individual versus community, short term versus long term, and justice versus mercy. Defining ethical dilemmas in these terms is difficult at first, but a frame work or process can be evolved to help us to define the problem and set up the testing of the problem against ethical standards. To define a problem in terms of 'right versus wrong' either implies defining a problem that is not an ethical dilemma. Or, worse yet, pre-defines the solution to the problem since one virtue or value is stated in a positive way while the other virtue or value is stated in a negative way.

Choices between black and white are easy and in any case it does not reach the top. It is this familiar shade of grey which oscillates between black and white that confronts us as leaders. As one expert once commented that there are approximately 260 shades of grey. To sort out such dilemmas, one is sometimes advised to keep a chronic idealist in the organization. This idealist could be trusted to be the voice of the conscience every time matters of principle are brought down into the dusty flats of earthly action. Conscience as they say is the best pillow to sleep on. This quite voice within all of us, indeed, becomes active and assertive when spirit is high, where a sustained effort is made to enlighten it and leadership by persuasion rules.

Moral Haze Confronting an Executive

Success is demanded of an executive. He must stay in office to exercise his function. Even if he and his family own the company, he must succeed in the competitive whirl, or there will be no company over which he may reign as an executive. Hence, a standard of success, which must derive ultimately from moral issues, becomes inevitable. The thoughtful businessman may wonder what test measures his success. Is it:

- Growth of his organization?
- Development of efficiency in production or services offered?
- Gain in good will toward the corporation?
- Extension of service to the public?

What are the hazards which no executive can bypass, jump over, or wave out of his way? I believe that one of the tests of an executive is his capacity to face the hazards and problems of:

- Living with the necessity of compromise, but never compromising too much.
- Being free to disclose only parts of the truth on many occasions, yet needing to see the whole truth.
- Having to make final decisions but on the basis of incomplete facts.
- Accepting responsibilities for the mistakes of subordinates while not allowing them to make too many mistakes.
- Living up to the image that the public and his associates demand of a man in high office, but not becoming the victim of it.
- Succeeding as a man of thought as well as a man of action.

Guide to Decision Making in An Ethical Arena

Decision making in an ethical ambience requires of individuals three qualities that can be identified and developed:

- The first is the competence to recognize ethical issues and to think through the consequence of alternative resolutions.
- The second is 'self-confidence' to seek out different points of view and then decide what is right at a given time and place in a particular set of relationships and circumstances.
- The third is what one would call 'tough-mindedness', which is the willingness to make decisions when all that needs to be known cannot be known and when the questions that press for answers have no established and incontrovertible solutions.

Three Alternative Bases for Decision Making

Once an actor has defined the problem in terms of 'right versus right' and identified the obvious courses of action, these courses of action should be tested against three completely different criteria for ethical decision making. They are: *principles or rules-based approach; consequences or the utilitarian approach; and virtues.* These are the three basic schools of thought for ethics, which are worthy of further examination or clarification.

Principles-based ethics

Immanuel Kant is the principal philosopher of this school of thought. Principle-based ethics is defined in many ways, but one general definition is that one should not act according to the consequences of an action, but instead according to agreed-upon or settled values and principles. When looking at ethical dilemmas through the 'lens' of principles or rule-based ethics, consideration must be made for the rules that exist or should exist. The consequences of actions are not considered, but the principles related to the actions one makes in response to the ethical dilemma. The imperative here is 'act as if the maxim of your action was to become a universal law of nature'. The key questions to ask when considering this principles or rules-based approach would be 'what rules exist' and 'what are my moral obligations'? Ethical acceptability stems from actions regardless of the consequences.

Consequence-based ethics

The second general basis for ethics is consequence-based ethics or utilitarianism, which is closely aligned with the philosopher John Stuart Mill. Ethical decisions determined under this basis are made on the likely consequences or results of the actions. Decisions are judged by their consequences depending on the results to be maximized - security, happiness, pleasure, dignity, and the like. When looking at ethical dilemmas through the 'lens' of consequence-based ethics, or utilitarianism, consideration must be made for who wins and who loses. The consequences of actions are the prime considerations. John Stuart Mill's diktat should help to focus the decisions made using this approach: 'Do what produces the greatest good for the greatest number'. Key questions to ask when considering the consequence-based ethics or utilitarianism would be 'what give the biggest bang for the buck' and 'who wins and losses?' In consequence-based ethics, the ethical acceptability is based on the consequence of actions. However, very often ethics such as these can be misused to justify wrongs.

Virtue-based ethics

Plato and Aristotle provided the first ethics theory – virtue, or in today's political language, 'character matters.'

The focus in virtue ethics is not on 'what one should do' but rather 'what kind of person one should be?' Good character or virtues is central to virtue theory. When looking at ethical dilemmas through the 'lens' of virtue-based ethics, consideration must be made for what a virtuous person would do. The golden rule can be used to focus the decisions made using this approach: 'Do to others what you would have them do to you.' Key questions to ask when considering virtues-based ethics would be.' 'what if I told someone I respect or told TV /Media audience-which option I have chosen', what would they say?' or 'what if my actions showed up on the front page of the newspaper?' In virtue theory, one concentrates on who a person 'ought to be' in contrast to other theories that concentrate on what a person 'ought to do'.

Figure 3. Ethical Triangle

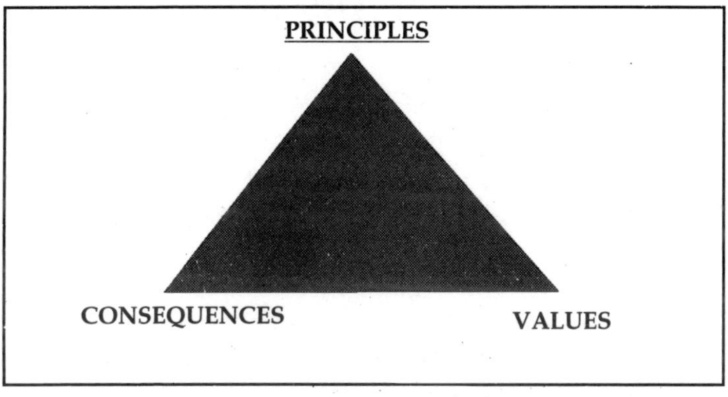

This is a graphic representation of the three premises which has been just described.

Which of the ethical philosophies are the most useful–principle or rule-based ethics, consequence or the utilitarian-based ethics, or virtue-based ethics? Which one of the philosophies is the best fit for human behavior? All three appear to have some merit; all three can be used for decision-making as distinct filters that reveal different aspects of a situation requiring an ethical choice. To consider only one of the different theoretical bases runs the risk of being one-sided in analysis. Whether principles, consequences, or virtue provide the true reasons for ethical decision making, all three of the theories and their lineages are useful for gaining insight into the complexity of ethical decision making.

A morally laden decision involves all three, the person responsible, the act, and the outcome. Professionally minded executives are well advised to take all the three perceptions into account. But remember, the responsibility for an action lies with us because our responsibilities derive from what we can control and the decisions we make.

Decision Making Model in an Ethical Ambience

A suggested model for a skillful ethical decision making could include the following steps:

- **Define the problem (ethical dilemma) in terms of right vs right**—The first step is to identify the problem, the ethical dilemma, in terms of right versus right. Again, this is necessary to provide clarity to the dilemma while ensuring that a pre-determined decision is not made. Stating the problem in this format will help to test the actions that should be taken. It implies getting the facts of the case, identifying the stake holders, ascertaining the nature of the issue with what is most efficient/ prudent, and if so how? Extensive fact gathering may also diffuse the emotionalism of an issue. A moral decision is an informed decision. A decision that is based on blind or convenient ignorance is hardly defensible.

- **Consider alternative courses of action**—The second step is to determine the possible actions. There will probably be two obvious responses - to do or not do. Of course, this is not the dilemma - these courses of actions are responses to the dilemma. It is important during this step to realize and even hope for a possible third alternative response to the dilemma. The questions that would need deliberation are:
    - What options are unacceptable and why? Are the value priorities or reasoning, flawed due to inadequacy or ambiguity of facts?
    - Are the major options limited by systemic constraints? Can they be challenged or changed?
- **Test the courses of action against the 'ethical triangle' namely, 'principle, consequence and virtue' based ethics**—The third step is to examine the two alternative courses of action through the lens of the three ethical systems. The most methodical means to do that is to first look through principles-based ethics, then consequences-based ethics, and finally through virtues-based ethics. Generally, the principles will be relatively easy, while the consequences will not be as easy, particularly when you look at all of the potential second and third order effects of actions. Because virtues-based ethics uses discretion to determine the 'golden mean', it can serve as the integrating approach to ethics. Here some of the questions that would need to be answered would include:
    - Which option will produce the most good and do the least harm?
    - Which option best respects the rights of all who have a stake?

- Which option leads me to act as the sort of person I want to be?

- Consider additional alternative courses of action (such as 'win-win' possibilities or no decision at all). The fourth step is to step back and see if a third response or an alternative course of action has presented itself (such as 'win-win' possibilities or no decision at all). Going through the process may indicate that there is another answer rather than the two courses of action initially determined. This will not always be true, but it is best to step back and see if there is another alternative. This would imply whether one has identified creative options.

- **Chose the course of action that best represents organization's values**—The fifth step is deciding a course of action. That choice should be made based upon an analysis using all three of the ethical systems, but, in the end, the choice is also made in the context of the organizational climate and culture as well as the professional values of the organization. The congruence of our stated values and our actual practices is pivotal to any organization's success.

- **Implement the course of action. The final step is implementation**—This is where the rubber meets the road; by this time, the choice should be well thought out. Executives are more than implementers of policy, they are also charged with support for the realization of democratic principles and commitment to obeying the law. This is particularly true when decisions need to be made quickly and when there is no 'top cover' guaranteed for the decisions made. Putting ethical decisions into action requires moral character.

There is yet another aspect to be considered after

acting on the decision one has taken, i.e. is to 'reflect on the outcome', in that, how did the decision turn out to be and what has one learned from this specific situation? Also, one has to reflect on whether the implemented decision has taken into consideration the concerns of all stake holders. Is there anything that you or your organization can do now to avoid recurrence of similar situation in future?

Conclusion

There is a need to discern if there is a crisis of conscience in actual situations where managers and executives face complex and arduous problems of ethics. The increasingly competitive business environment has resulted in an environment where many executives and managers are subjected to tests of conscience for which they are ill prepared, indeed, for which there may be no preparation. It has become increasingly difficult for them to act their individual parts well and still retain free and clear consciences.

Modern day executives and managers are often faced with situations where they are required to commit themselves, either openly or tacitly, to an action they may not agree with. They may be participating, willingly or unwillingly, in activities that are normally cloudy, questionable from a business point of view, and perhaps, of doubtful legality. The subject is not that the acts are patently illegal, or where the responsibility is specific and detailed, or where the facts are clear-cut and defined. Rather, the issues, are generally involving unclear, undefined areas of activity where by association, an individual is involved in a course of action that he believes--not necessarily knows--is wrong. Such crises of conscience raise the issue of the correct course of action for executives and managers who are confronted with accepting questionable conduct of their superiors by being expected either to agree to it or to close their eyes to it.

Many organizations and business today have realized the power of shared values and have worked to become more value-based. Leadership-based shared missions and values create true commitment. Incentives, bonuses, stock options, and other rewards for good behavior cannot take the place of principled leadership. If motivation in our organization is based on carrots and sticks, the organization is always at the mercy of those who can offer more or bigger carrots. And, sticks can, at best, ensure compliance but not commitment. As executives, consider actions that you should take that can build and not destroy commitment. Do you put yourself ahead of the company, even as you talk about mission and values and the worth and dignity of all your people? It is not hard for people to sense the contrast between language and behavior, for after all, actions do speak louder than words. And we cannot expect people to be truly committed to the success of those whose vision does not extend much further than personal advancement.

It has been my attempt to put across to you some of my views on this subject. It was not my intention to provide to you definitive rules for executive choices when right or wrong are confusingly entangled. Judgment-free formulas do not appear here. I am sure each one of you with your rich experience will carry out fresh appraisals of your own situations and discern courses of action that can convert good intentions into good results. In order to have an ethical consciousness we should all be aware of our personal fallibility. Of course, there is a limit to how much a declared code or even regulation can do.

In the final analysis, one can write down all the rules, pass resolutions in appropriate bodies, but conformity remains doubtful. Ultimately, there has to be a philosophy of ethical behavior that should come from the way human beings operate in a professional manner. The executive must manage his life so that he can fill up his mind with interesting ideas that supply a context and guide for his actions. The thoughtful executive comes at last to face the ultimate question of whether he is big enough for his office. If he is, it will be in a large measure because he is adequately prepared to deal with the moral issues put before him.

Index